Pass English Comp

The Study Guide for Critical Thinking, Rhetoric, and College Writing

Pass English Comp

The Study Guide for Critical Thinking, Rhetoric, and College Writing

Susan Ferguson

Ninth Month Publishing Co.
Sedona, Arizona

Pass English Comp: The Study Guide for Critical Thinking, Rhetoric, and College Writing

© 2008 by Susan Ferguson

200 pages.
First edition includes bibliographic references and index.
ISBN-13:   978-0-9822271-0-7

Published by
Ninth Month Publishing Co.
365 Northview Road
Sedona AZ 86336
(928) 225-0271

Manufactured in the United States of America.

Illustration Credits
Cover art: © iStockphoto.com/cyrop (Cyro Pintos)
Tattoo woman: © iStockphoto.com/webphotographeer (Lidija Tomic)
Woman with keys: © Crestock.com/togir (Tormod Rossavik)
Model in feather boa: © Crestock.com/zdenkamicka (Zdenka Micka)
Woman in lingerie: © Crestock.com/zdenkamicka (Zdenka Micka)
Soldier statue: © iStockphoto.com/cathyclapper2 (Cathleen Clapper)
Fireman: © iStockphoto.com/DanielBendjy (Daniel Bendjy)
Car on road: © iStockphoto.com/wbritten (William Britten)
Face icons: © iStockphoto.com/TheFlyingSaucer (Attila Kis)

D9-10 BT 23.96

Book Design: Susan Ferguson   09-10

The Internet website addresses listed in the text were correct at the time of publication. Inclusion of a website does not represent endorsement by the author or Ninth Month Publishing Co. Ninth Month Publishing Co. does not guarantee the accuracy of the information at the websites mentioned in the text.

Visit www.passenglishcomp.com for more information about this book.

To Lynn, Justin, and Shannon –

for your love, encouragement, patience, and support.

For everything.

Table of Contents

About the Author

Susan Ferguson is a native of St. Louis, Missouri. Before embarking on a writing career, she was a student, a farmer, a greenhouse manager, a florist, and a mom. She completed her undergraduate education at Missouri Western State University and worked as a journalist for nearly ten years before venturing into the world of marketing. Her natural curiosity about everything besides the task she was assigned to at the time led her into the worlds of graphic design and publishing, where she has worked as an independent editor, book designer, and writer since 1995. Her work has been recognized by the Missouri Press Association, Missouri Writers Guild, and National Council on Crime and Delinquency. In 2008 she completed a Master of Arts degree in English-Creative Writing at Northern Arizona University. She lives in Sedona, Arizona, where she is working on numerous writing projects and helping others learn to write.

Acknowledgements

I owe so much to the men and women who have helped make this book a reality. The first thank you goes to Lynn Lindhurst for everything wonderful that he does to make writing a serious pursuit and life a joy. Hugs and thanks go to my children, Shannon and Justin, for their unceasing support and encouragement, and to my brother, Ken, for listening and offering ideas. Thanks, too, to Gregory Dobie for his encouragement and suggestions. To my fellow teaching assistants Luke Reynolds, Jenn McArdle, Dave Kopp, Mackenzie Kell, Brent Webster, Nick Tambakeras, Daniel J. Pinney, Brooke Wonders, Leah Rogin-Roper, Jeff Ortiz, Rachel Meth, Isaac Melum, Patty Petelin, and Kyle Boggs – much gratitude for helping to construct some sort of logic out of chaos during our years in grad school. Thanks to Sibylle Gruber, Laura Gray-Rosendale, Jane Woodman, Tara Green, Steve Rosendale, Monica Brown, Ann Cummins, and Paul Ferlazzo, who, as my professors and mentors, taught me how to create my own path. Finally, an enormous thank you to all of my former students at Northern Arizona University for their patience and suggestions that helped make English 105 bearable for all of us. No students were deliberately harmed in the making of this book.

Susan Ferguson
December 2008

Introduction

You don't have to be a brilliant student to be admitted to a college or university. You don't even have to be a great student to be accepted to a college. Brilliance and greatness help, as you have discovered as you have applied to umpteen schools, but brilliance and greatness are not required. In fact, evidence of brilliance and greatness can be anomalies in some college admissions offices. After all, lots of college applicants are young. They haven't had the chance to achieve the greatness they're due. They're lacking a few skills; they're short on technical know-how; many aren't even sure what they want to do or be when they grow up. That's why they are applying to college.

The university where I taught English composition for two years considered a 2.0 GPA in each of six core competency areas the acceptable minimum standard for admission to the school's undergraduate programs (Northern Arizona University). In many education systems, a 2.0 GPA is equivalent to a C. You know what a C means. Attached to an assignment or exam, a C grade indicates that the work therein is average or mediocre – good enough to get you into college but certainly not good enough to keep you there.

In order to stay in college, your work cannot be average. In order to stay in college, you and your work have to become great, or if you're really motivated, brilliant. You can't just coast on mediocrity for two, four, six, or eight years on your way to becoming whatever you dream of being. Coasting costs lots of money, yields little, and frequently can move you further away from the level of success you hoped to reach. In order to stay in college – in order to succeed in college – you have to be great. You have to be proactive. You have to work. You have to apply your mind and body to meet the challenges of academia so that your level of understanding, your abilities, and your skills are constantly improving. Improvement carries you closer to greatness, and greatness carries you closer to brilliance and the goals and success you want to attain. With greatness, you eventually graduate and take on the world, where, as much as I hate to say it, the process of moving from average to great to brilliant starts all over again.

So, what does any of this have to do with English composition and this book? In a nutshell: When you can think critically and communicate information and ideas effectively in your writing, you can move from mediocrity to greatness and on to brilliance. You possess the skills you need to achieve your goals. The goal of *Pass English Comp* as a study guide is to help you learn to think critically and write effectively. *Pass English Comp* was created to help you develop skills and improve your understanding of critical thinking, rhetoric, and writing – ostensibly for college but also for all the years after that.

Pass English Comp is not a dry, crusty textbook with page after page of dry, crusty essays and dry, crusty analysis and dry, crusty questions at the end of every dry, crusty chapter that you have to choke down like day-old cornbread and read and answer before tomorrow's dry, crusty class. *Pass English Comp* is an informal collection of ideas, diagrams, and charts; an eclectic assortment of curious essays and articles; a few reflective exercises; and a plethora of semicolons that will help you better understand the concepts of critical thinking, rhetoric, and college writing. You can dive in wherever you need to for tips and suggestions that will help you. That way, you'll be able to pass English Comp (or Fundamentals of Composition or Freshman Composition or English 1 or English 105 or Logic and Rhetoric or whatever they call it at your school) and carry with you forever the concepts for use in other classes and in everyday life. This book contains information about college writing, rhetoric, and critical thinking that is often otherwise lost in the much larger, more complicated, less pleasant and hardly exact science of that non-scientific subject called English composition. If you understand the concepts and techniques presented in *Pass English Comp,* you will be more likely to achieve greatness through improved abilities and skills in critical thinking, rhetoric, and writing. Your grades may improve, as well. That's it, in a nutshell.

It would be great if you started at the beginning of the book and read it to the end. That way you would learn more than you otherwise would if you just read enough to get by. But you're probably up to your ears in things that people would like you to read from beginning to end, and you're probably not sure how much spare time you have to read one more book. If you have time, start at page 1. If you don't have time, use the table of contents and the index to search for the information you need. Then, when you do have a few spare minutes, read a whole chapter or section.

As you read this book, pay attention to the notations in the page margins. The notations offer insights into the text and provide additional information that you will find helpful in understanding an idea or a process. The margins also have plenty of room for you to make your own notations. The exercises in this book are designed to encourage you to reflect and write about the text you have just read. A few of the questions have right and wrong answers; most require contemplative consideration. Either way, I encourage you to write out your responses. Good writers know that writing reinforces understanding. It's also good practice for the moment when you have to put words on paper.

Thinking and Learning

Making the Transition from Wherever-You-Were to College 1

Think about what you were doing with your life six months ago. Maybe you were in high school or taking classes at the community college, working at a job, serving in the military or on a religious mission, or just hanging around at your parents' house, waiting for your friends to call so you could go hang out at somebody else's house for a while.

Whatever the scenario, there's a good chance that your life required some form of communicating ideas and information. If you were in school, maybe that meant researching and writing papers for your classes. If you were at work, maybe you had to make an eye-catching sign advertising "All Candy Bars – 20% Off" or tell a customer that tonight's specials included a walnut-crusted sea bass or a Ricotta cheese-stuffed red pepper, each with green salad and bread. If you were in the military, maybe you were listening to instructions from your commander to be at a specific location at a specific time to await further orders. If you were on a religious mission, maybe you were answering a question about the significance of light in your religion's teachings. Even if you were just hanging around the house waiting for your friends to call, there's a good chance that whatever they asked you in that phone call was stated in such a way that it appealed to you emotionally and you had to decide whether the payoff was good enough for you to put on shoes and walk or drive over to their house to do whatever it was they asked you to do.

Critical thinking skills would have been necessary in each of these scenarios. You might have even used such skills without knowing what they were. Now that you're in college, thinking critically is absolutely essential because you're being bombarded 24/7 with stuff from every direction. In addition to the stuff you're hearing in your classes, you're constantly receiving information and ideas from your parents, siblings, friends, roommates, church, social groups, television, the news media, movies, music, video games, books, magazines, exhibits, theater, businesses, and the Internet. If you're a busy person, you don't have time to analyze all of it. More than likely, you just store it away in your brain and it pops up later in some form that you haven't given much thought to. As you develop the skills to think critically, you will be more able to analyze and filter the information that's put in front of you in order to discern its validity. Thinking critically helps you to cut down on the mental clutter and see patterns and relationships in the information you choose to store.

You probably didn't do much discerning of information while you were in school or at your job or wherever you were six months ago. Your teachers or boss probably told you what to do and think while you were in school or working, and your parents and friends told you what to do and think the rest of the time. When you got tired of listening to everybody, you escaped into a movie or video game or music, where maybe you didn't realize it but a director or videographer or musician was using his or her skills to tell you what to do and think. Being the dutiful person you were, you took it all in, hanging on every word because they came from sources you liked or hung out with or had to listen to. When you finally got tired of all of the noise, you escaped into sleep, where your brain took a break from all of the input and started sorting out in its own miraculous way which information it wanted to keep and which info it wanted to discard. More than likely, your brain retained the information from the memories that were most pleasant and most unpleasant for you emotionally, turning them into thoughts that helped you to learn certain behaviors. The end result of all of this mental activity is that you have accumulated a brain full of information and ideas from various influential sources. In short: You are the sum total of every idea and piece of information that has bombarded you. However, because you have probably not yet learned to think as critically as you should, this brain full of information and ideas is like a giant thrift store in your head – cluttered and unorganized, jammed full of factoids and bits and pieces of memories, and brimming with recollections of your reactions, confusing ideas, and sentimental pap that doesn't mean anything to anybody (and a lot of times that includes you).

In college, your professors will expect you to do a lot of discerning. They will bombard you with information in the forms of lectures, readings, handouts, presentations, and so on, just like your teachers did in high school. They will focus, and ask you to focus, on a particular subject so closely that you feel like you are drowning or smothering in American history or cultural anthropology or English comp or whatever the class is. They will insist that you respect, if not adopt, their particular ideological bent or academic passion, at least for the duration of the semester so you can appreciate not only their wisdom and methodology but also all the untold intellectual suffering they had to endure to earn that Ph.D. that so righteously hangs on their office wall. (Don't misunderstand. There's a lot of untold intellectual suffering on the way to an advanced degree. Anybody who completes a doctorate or a master's degree deserves to be respected.) As you focus, and respect, and adopt, you will find yourself discerning while you are in the shower, while you're skateboarding to class, while you're eating cheese curls and drinking coffee before you go to bed at 3 AM. You will become a discerning fool.

And that's just the first week of college. Life gets more intense as the semester wears on.

You're not in high school any more

When I was teaching, I observed that my freshman students spent the first four weeks or so of their first semester comparing their college classroom situation to their experiences in high school. Students were always saying, "In high school, we had to_____" or "Our high school teacher made us _____" or "We studied something like this in high school, but I don't remember what it meant." As the students sat in the classroom each day – each of them observing the behavior of their fellow students, struggling to keep up with study expectations at a pace they could not control, meting out questions and answers a word at a time so as to not embarrass themselves – I realized that everything about the students' first semester in college must be so overwhelmingly unfamiliar that they were searching frantically through their brains to find any scrap of memory that remotely resembled something in the chaos they were experiencing. When they found it, they blurted out: "In high school, we had to _____" as if to say, "Thank goodness! I *have* seen this somewhere! It's not as crazy unfamiliar chaotic as it seems."

College life can be discombobulating. The living arrangements, meals, scheduling, bureau-cracy, teachers' expectations, recreation options, financial obligations, social activities, personal responsibilities – your first semester of college dumps a whole new way of living on you within a few fast-paced weeks. Coping with these rapid-fire, often disorienting changes in your social, financial, and emotional life can be a full-time job all by itself, but that's just a part of the challenge of college. You are also expected to buckle down, hit the books, concentrate, and perform well academically. Unfortunately, signing the papers to go from Wherever-You-Were to College didn't automatically grant you any special superhuman powers. You still have to cope, be flexible, study, be responsible, socialize, take care of your body and mind, pay your bills, and keep your parents happy – all at the same time. It's a lot of work.

It's no wonder that so many average students don't survive their first semester. Ill-equipped to discern the difference between choices and obligations, the average student struggles with system overload, trying to get by with ordinary work while searching desperately to find some shred of familiarity in this new environment. Every time I heard a student say, "But in high school we had to _____," I translated that to, "Help me. I'm drowning. Somebody throw me a rope."

By the fifth or sixth week of the first semester, the chants in the classroom began to change. Students were getting to know their fellow students, the initial shock about college coursework was fading, their parents weren't calling as much, and campus living had acquired some consistency. They acknowledged that the obligations closely tied to the necessities of food, clothing, and shelter had to be met, but there was the occasional spare minute to breathe and relax. Yet, while many aspects of college life were becoming more familiar, students were still somewhat reluctant to make the mental shift from Wherever-You-Were to College.

This was the time in the semester when the familiar expression "In high school we had to _____" changed to the more ominous "This sure isn't like what we did in high school." Students who clung to the high-school mindset continued to ask if they could receive extra credit for showing up for a class where attendance was required. (Words of advice: Don't be this student. Ever.) When they were instructed to write down during class five key ideas reflected in that day's reading because no one in class wanted to actually discuss the reading, they wanted to know how many points their response would be worth to their grades. That other familiar expression, "Our high school teacher used to make us do _____," changed to "You didn't tell us we had to do _____," which clearly indicated to me that some students were still stuck in Wherever-You-Were, still looking for someone besides themselves to be responsible for the burden of school. A few students had moved beyond that point, but many still clung to the dream of Wherever-You-Were because there was no clear incentive to make the leap.

Midterm grades changed all that. By the end of the eighth week of the first semester, students had probably taken a midterm examination or turned in a paper that counted significantly toward their final grade in the course. That midterm grade was a real eye-opener. If it was a good grade, a student might have remarked, "Wow, this sure isn't like high school," meaning, "I'm beginning to see the difference between where I was six months ago and where I am now. I better get to work." I used to get all warm and tingly when I heard that from a student with a good midterm grade, because it meant that he or she was making headway out of Wherever-You-Were and into College. This student got it. This student, however mediocre he or she might have been in the months prior to college, was on the way to greatness. This student had figured out what it would take to go far.

If, however, I heard the same remark, "Wow, this sure isn't like high school," from the student with the lousy grade, I had mixed feelings. While the unhappy tone implied that the student recognized his or her dilemma, the lousy grade suggested that the student wasn't yet ready to shoulder his responsibilities as a college student. He was still blaming his teacher, or the course, or the textbook, or his roommate, or the dorm food – he was blaming anybody and anything but himself for his predicament. He didn't get it. His potential was unclear – to him as well as to me. His future did not look bright.

Fortunately, most semesters are only sixteen weeks. The agony and frustration of transition can only last so long. The student with the good midterm grade reflected on the actions taken thus far and continued to build on those experiences in order to move from average to greatness. The student with the good midterm grade did whatever he or she needed to do during the next eight weeks to pass the class.

The student with the lousy grade wasn't quite so self-aware. His or her reflections about what had happened since the start of the semester were likely to be rather spotty, vague, or unclear. His efforts hadn't produced anything that felt rewarding or created incentive. (As you likely already know, it's difficult to feel positive about random, disjointed, dissatisfying experiences.) This student had a couple of options: He or she could accept responsibility for his situation and his academic tasks and use the next eight weeks to bring his grades up, or he could party like crazy while he invented excuses to offer to the parents when he crashed and burned at the end of the semester.

Many people enter college unprepared and with some degree of apprehension; maybe you are one of them. This is, after all, a new experience, and there will be many situations when you will wish you had a mentor or role model to guide you through it. As you tackle the day-to-day tasks, you will discover that you either have the wherewithal and fortitude to do these tasks well, or to your dismay, you will realize that you have a tendency to procrastinate or to wait for someone else to do the tasks for you. Curiously, college doesn't provide servants or clones. When you accept the school's invitation to attend in order to pursue a degree, you agree to do the work yourself and complete the requirements the school sets out for you. In order to do that, you have to be willing to make a positive transition from Wherever-You-Were to College – the sooner the better. How you make the transition is up to you. Here are a few recommendations that may make things go more smoothly.

Open-mindedness helps

Be receptive to new ideas, listen, and be flexible and open-minded rather than rigid and judgmental. Try to avoid becoming stressed about everything unfamiliar. In college, you will meet lots of new people and hear information and ideas that you would have never heard when you were in Wherever-You-Were. While you don't have to embrace every new idea presented to you, you will have a more positive learning experience if you recognize that 1) the world in which you live is made up of many bits of information, 2) the delivery of this information is influenced by perspective, and 3) some of this information is worth your consideration. If you cling only to the information and ideas presented to you when you were a child and become defensive and reject anything that differs from your childhood understanding, you will have a difficult time making sense of some of the new information that comes your way. Developing the skills to think critically and communicate effectively will help you to make sense of the new stuff. Add to that your new knowledge about particular subjects, and you will be able to decide for yourself whether to accept or reject new ideas.

Figure 1 may help you appreciate the concept of perspective. Imagine you are out walking and you stumble across a group of people sitting in a circle around a statue of a soldier. The soldier is holding a gun in his left hand and raising his right hand into the air. One of his legs is bent. Each viewer has been instructed to look straight ahead, interpret, and describe only the portion of the soldier that is visible. Viewer 1, directly in front of the statue, can see the soldier's face, his uniform, the upraised hand, and the gun. Viewer 2, to the right of Viewer 1, can't see the soldier's face clearly but can see the left side of the uniform and the gun. Viewer 3, next to Viewer 2, can see the back of the soldier, his backpack, and the gun but can't see the soldier's face. Viewer 4, beside Viewer 3, can see the back of the soldier but can't see the face and can't tell what the soldier is holding in his upraised hand. Viewer 5, next to Viewer 4, can see the right side of the soldier but can't clearly see the soldier's face; it looks like the soldier might be lifting his gun. Viewer 6, next to Viewer 5, can see the soldier's uniform, his face, and the gun.

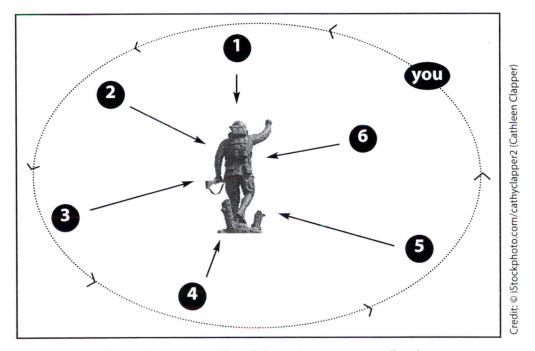

Credit: © iStockphoto.com/cathyclapper2 (Cathleen Clapper)

Figure 1 Perspective is influenced by the viewer's knowledge and experience, as well as the unique vantage point from which a viewer "sees" a subject. In this case, a prior knowledge of soldiers influences the interpretations of viewers 1-6, who can see the soldier only from their unique vantage point. You are the only person able to move around the statue, viewing it from all vantage points to form a more accurate interpretation.

If you ask each viewer to interpret and describe the statue based only on what he or she sees, you will hear many different descriptions based on each viewer's experience and knowledge of statues and soldiers. Some responses might be:

"The angry soldier is running towards something to fight with it." (Viewer 1)

"The brave soldier is threatening the enemy." (Viewer 6)

"The soldier is raising his gun to fight with something." (Viewer 5)

"The man in the uniform is jumping off a fence to escape from something." (Viewer 4)

"The soldier is raising his fist in victory." (Viewers 2 & 3)

Each viewer perceives the statue, and its message, differently because of his or her unique perspective. No single interpretation is right or wrong; it just is. Collectively, these descriptions incorporate several perspectives that work together to create what the people in the group clearly recognize is the image, and the idea, of a soldier.

The same thing happens in the classroom when students are discussing ideas. One student may have one perception of a reading assignment, while another student has a different interpretation or perspective. A third student has another interpretation, and another student, yet another interpretation. These interpretations and perspectives help to form the overall message of the reading. There is no single right interpretation and single wrong interpretation, and nothing in between. There are instead several interpretations based on individual perspectives. Listening to the different perspectives can open doors to new ways of thinking and understanding.

Time management is a good thing

If you have never had to manage your own schedule, now is the time to start: plan your day or week *before* it happens, schedule your study time and play time, and give yourself time to complete the activities you schedule. A good rule of thumb for planning your studies is to allow three hours of study time for every hour of class time. I know; that sounds outrageous. Who wants to spend fifty to sixty hours a week slaving over readings, homework, and research after spending sixteen to eighteen hours in the classroom?

Maybe it will help to look at your situation this way: Every credit hour in which you are enrolled during a semester costs you money. When you enroll in college, you agree to pay the college a specific amount of money for a given amount of information that the college has to "sell" to you to help you get an academic degree so that you presumably can succeed in a given career field. When you take a class one time, study hard, and get a passing grade, you have completed the "money for information" transaction in its simplest and most economical way. If, however, you take a class the first time but don't study hard and don't get a passing grade, you will probably have to take the class a second time in order to meet the school's requirements for graduation. That means you will have to spend twice as much money to receive the same information. That makes your education much more expensive without any added value. That's not wise. Planning sufficient study time is the much wiser path to choose.

Another tip that may help you survive the pace of college involves planning your semester workload using the "Wall of Work." For this project, you need a blank wall or door, a short stack of copy paper (or index cards or sticky notes), a roll of tape, a few colored markers, and the syllabi for your classes. To complete this project, select a marker of a specific color to represent a specific class. Using the marker and your syllabus for that class, write each assignment on a separate sheet of paper, along with the course number, and the date it's due in that class, like "Eng 644-Byerly response paper-March 7." Select a different color marker for your second class and do the same thing: write on a separate sheet of copy paper each assignment, the course number, and the date that it's due. Create assignment sheets for all of your classes. Then put these assignment sheets in order according to the due date. If you have two or three papers due on a single date and you want to shift one of them back a day or two, now's the time to do it. Write the revised date on the assignment sheet. Then take the sheets and hang them side by side in rows in due-date order on your expanse of blank wall.

The sheets will consume a lot of wall space – hence the name "Wall of Work" – but you will have at a glance the workload of your entire semester laid out in front of you in such a way that your wall becomes your semester calendar, your reason for being. Each time you complete an assignment, tear off the assignment sheet and throw it away.

At the start of my last semester of grad school, I hung 56 assignment sheets on my closet doors. Nothing gave me greater satisfaction than to finish an assignment, rip that assignment sheet off the wall, wad it up, and toss it into the trash. Not that there was anything particularly aesthetic about the closet doors underneath, but it was a great feeling to tear down that last assignment sheet and see those blank white panels again.

Stay healthy

Take care of your body and brain. Try to go to bed at the same time every night and get up at the same time every morning so that your body doesn't get exhausted and become more susceptible to illness. Pay attention to the nature and quality of the stuff you eat and drink; nutritious foods and drinks will give you more mental and physical energy than foods packaged in cellophane and/or sold in vending machines. If you have no idea what a nutritious food is, do some research on the Internet and at the grocery store. While the "freshman fifteen" theory isn't fully documented, there is evidence that first-year students do experience weight gains that can be avoided through an understanding of basic nutrition, meal management, and exercise. Manage your stress levels by taking part in physical activity that will generate endorphins to help you feel better. Bear in mind that you have your whole life ahead of you to kill your brain cells with chemicals; there is no urgency about trying to kill them all in one night or weekend. If you can afford it, go home occasionally and talk with your friends, parents, and grandparents about what you're learning in school. Don't be surprised if your old friends seem to behave a bit differently when you're around them; you and your friends may be growing in different directions now that you're in college. Again, appreciate and respect the differences and enjoy the interests you share in common.

Lastly, enjoy the opportunities that college presents. I'm not just talking about hanging out with friends; friends are a good thing, but they aren't everything. Get involved with organizations and activities that expand your knowledge and interests. If you think you want to know more about politics or community activism, volunteer with a political or social service organization on campus or in the community. If you are curious about a particular kind of exercise, join a fitness group or recreation club so you can see if that activity is right for you. If you have a creative or artistic side, develop your talents in a theater or music group. Whether you want to become the nation's next top CEO or the best counselor on the planet, pursue internships and training opportunities that your school offers through its student life and academic departments. Take an interest in the world beyond the walls of the college or university you're attending. After all, it won't be too many more years until you are living out there again.

College opens all sorts of doors for the student who takes advantage of the opportunities therein. Critical thinking and effective communication through writing will help you evaluate and express your interpretations of the ideas and information you discover.

What Do You Know? **2**

The activity you know as writing has experienced a lot of educational changes during the past thirty years. What used to be an activity that focused on production of an end product – completion of a letter, research paper, book report, or presentation – and was steeped in rules about form, grammar, spelling, and punctuation has permutated into an activity that focuses on process, functionality, and the writer's style. Gone are the days when conventions dominated the world of writing. The conventions are still there; they just don't command as much attention as they once did. Now, teachers at the middle and high school levels focus on helping the student understand the process – all the steps, stages, and elements to take into consideration that influence the ultimate outcome of the finished product. Writing is no longer all about rules but is instead rather touchy-feely and personal. Writing is "all about you" now, instead of "all about the rules." I can still hear the voices of my teacher peers in a workshop seven years ago as they explained how they encouraged their students to write by saying, "The important thing is that you said it, not why or how you did it."

Alas, writing conventions are still important. *Why* and *how* are still important. If, for example, you don't understand the function of the comma, then you won't understand how and why to use it correctly, and random words on your paper will look as if they have sprouted tiny tails. If you don't understand that the purpose of a research paper is to argue the validity of a claim by using documented scholarly research, then you won't understand why you have to do the research and how to document what you find. You have to have a good knowledge of the rules of writing in order to succeed at conveying your message.

If that's true, then what's the point of understanding the process? Academicians have stated that teaching the writing process puts the emphasis on *understanding* rather than on the *finished product*. I'll suggest that it's important to understand both the process and the conventions of the finished product. If you can understand the steps of writing *and* the rules, along with the different elements and purposes of writing, there's a good chance that you will be able to communicate your idea more effectively than you would if you just go through a lot of motions to produce what you hope is somebody else's notion of a finished product.

State boards of education establish student performance standards in several core competency areas. These standards define specific skill and knowledge expectations that the student must demonstrate in order to graduate from one grade and move on to the next. These standards may vary from state to state, but the expectations are essentially similar. The Arizona Board of Education's Writing Standard identifies several performance standards in writing for twelfth-grade students. In theory, a student graduating from high school will possess specific knowledge in each of three categories: Writing Process, Writing Elements, and Writing Applications. The charts presented on the next six pages contain terms and activities that your college instructors will assume you know. My intention here is not to reinvent your high school English education. Like your professors, I'm assuming you have learned these things already. If you haven't, now is your chance. If the terms are not familiar, look them up in a dictionary or review them on a website that provides information about college writing. Compare your knowledge and skills against the performance objectives listed in the charts.

Five distinct stages or steps of writing are identified in the Writing Process category. These include **prewriting, drafting, revising, editing,** and **publishing.** You may have heard teachers use other terms such as brainstorming, mind mapping, diagramming, outlining, reviewing, proofreading, and formatting to identify these stages. Performance objectives for each of the stages – things you should have known to pass the twelfth grade – are provided here for your review.

STAGE 1: PREWRITING
Prewriting is the planning stage, where you think about a topic, research it, and start organizing your thoughts. Prewriting includes using strategies to generate, plan, and organize ideas for specific purposes such as an essay, research paper, letter, story, play, or report.

_____**Generate ideas** through a variety of activities (e.g., brainstorming, mind mapping, diagramming, notes and logs, graphic organizers, record of writing ideas and discussion, printed material, or other sources).

_____**Determine the purpose** (e.g., to entertain, to inform, to communicate, to persuade, to explain) of an intended writing piece.

_____**Determine the intended audience** of a writing piece.

_____**Establish a controlling idea** appropriate to the type of writing.

_____**Use organizational strategies** (e.g., outline, chart, table, graph, Venn diagram, web, story map, plot pyramid) to plan writing.

_____**Maintain a record** (e.g., lists, journals, folders, notebooks) of writing ideas.

_____**Use time management strategies,** when appropriate, to produce a writing product within a set time period.

STAGE 2: DRAFTING
Drafting is the physical act of writing your ideas into organized groups of words. Drafting incorporates prewriting activities to create a first draft containing necessary elements for a specific purpose.

_____**Identify a purpose** for your writing.

_____**Develop a thesis statement** that expresses the purpose of your writing.

_____**Use a prewriting plan** to develop the main idea(s) with supporting details.

_____**Sequence ideas** into a cohesive, meaningful order.

Source: Arizona Department of Education

STAGE 3: REVISING

Revising involves a review of the draft with the intention of making additions, corrections, and changes where these things need to be made. Revising includes evaluating and refining the rough draft for clarity and effectiveness. (Ask: Does this draft say what you want it to say?)

_____**Evaluate the draft** for use of ideas and content, organization, voice, word choice, and sentence fluency.

_____**Add details to the draft** to more effectively accomplish the purpose.

_____**Delete irrelevant and/or redundant information** from the draft to more effectively accomplish the purpose.

_____**Rearrange words, sentences, and paragraphs** in the draft in order to clarify the meaning or to enhance the writing style.

_____**Add transitional words and phrases** to the draft in order to clarify meaning or enhance the writing style.

_____**Use a variety of sentence structures** (i.e., simple, compound, complex) to improve sentence fluency in the draft.

_____**Apply appropriate tools or strategies** (e.g., peer review, checklists, rubrics) to refine the draft.

_____**Use resources and reference materials** (e.g., thesaurus, dictionary) to select more effective and precise language.

STAGE 4: EDITING

Editing is the process of correcting and changing grammar, punctuation, and spelling errors that might hamper the message of a paper. Editing includes proofreading and correcting the draft for conventions.

_____**Identify punctuation, spelling, and grammar and usage errors** in the draft.

_____**Use resources** (e.g., dictionary, word lists, spelling/grammar checkers) to correct conventions.

_____**Apply proofreading marks** to indicate errors in conventions.

_____**Apply appropriate strategies** (e.g., peer review, checklists, rubrics) to edit the draft.

STAGE 5: PUBLISHING

Publishing involves formatting and presenting a final product for the intended audience.

_____**Prepare writing that follows a format** appropriate for the purpose (e.g., for display, sharing with others, submitting to a publication).

_____**Include** techniques such as **principles of design** (e.g., margins, tabs, spacing, columns) and **graphics** (e.g., drawings, charts, graphs), when applicable, to enhance the final product.

_____**Write legibly.**

Source: Arizona Department of Education

In the Writing Elements category, the emphasis is on **ideas, voice, organization, word choice, sentence fluency,** and **conventions.** This curious assortment of terms sounds rather incongruous at first, but when they are all lumped together, they represent "how you say what you say when you write." *Ideas,* of course, refer to the information you select to include in your writing. The term *voice* relates to the tone of your writing: Is your writing formal and stiff (dry and crusty), or is it casual and easy to read? *Organization* focuses on the structure of your work and how your structure works with the other elements to present information; it is closely related to *fluency*, which concentrates on sentence structure and the flow of ideas in your writing. The term *conventions* refers to those things your parents and grandparents called the rules of grammar, spelling, and punctuation. *Word choice* is just what it sounds like: your usage of words and terms to convey ideas and information.

IDEAS AND CONTENT
Effective use of ideas and content means that the writing is clear and focused, holding the reader's attention throughout. Main ideas stand out and are developed by strong support and rich details. Purpose is accomplished.

_____**Maintain a clear, narrow focus** to support the topic.

_____**Write with an identifiable purpose** and for a specific audience.

_____**Provide sufficient, relevant, and carefully selected details** for support.

_____**Demonstrate a thorough, balanced explanation** of the topic.

_____**Include ideas and details** that show original perspective and insights.

VOICE
Voice will vary according to the type of piece but should be appropriately formal or casual, distant or personal, depending on the audience and purpose.

_____**Show awareness of the audience** through word choice, style, and an appropriate connection with, or distance from, the audience.

_____**Convey a sense of identity** through originality, sincerity, liveliness, or humor appropriate to topic and type of writing.

_____**Choose appropriate voice** (e.g., formal, informal, academic discourse) for the application.

_____**Use engaging and expressive language** that shows a commitment to the topic.

_____**Use language appropriate** to purpose, topic, and audience.

SENTENCE FLUENCY
Fluency addresses the rhythm and flow of language.

_____**Use a variety of sentence structures** (simple, compound, complex, and compound-complex) and lengths to reinforce relationships among ideas and to enhance the flow of the writing.

_____**Show extensive variation in sentence** beginnings, lengths, and patterns to enhance the flow of the writing.

_____**Demonstrate a flow** that is **natural and powerful** when read aloud.

Source: Arizona Department of Education

ORGANIZATION
Organization addresses the structure of the writing and integrates the central meaning and patterns that hold the piece together.

_____**Use a structure that fits the type of writing** (e.g., letter format, narrative, play, essay).

_____**Include a strong beginning** or introduction that draws in the reader.

_____**Place details appropriately** to support the main idea.

_____**Use effective transitions** among all elements (sentences, paragraphs, and ideas).

_____**Employ a variety of paragraphing strategies** (e.g., topical, chronological, spatial) appropriate to application and purpose.

_____**Create an ending** that provides a **sense of resolution** or closure.

CONVENTIONS
Conventions address the mechanics of writing, including capitalization, punctuation, spelling, grammar, usage, and paragraph breaks.

_____**Use capitals correctly** for proper nouns such as holidays, place/regional names, languages, historical events, organizations, academic courses (e.g., algebra/Algebra I), product names, words used as names, literary titles, titles, abbreviations, and proper adjectives.

_____**Use commas correctly** to punctuate items in a series; greetings and closings of letters; introductory words, phrases, and clauses; direct address; interruptors; compound sentences; appositives; and dialogue.

_____**Use quotation marks** to punctuate dialogue, titles, and exact words from sources.

_____**Use underlining or italics** to correctly identify titles and names of ships, spacecrafts, planes, and trains.

_____**Use colons** to punctuate business letter salutations and sentences introducing lists.

_____**Use semicolons** to punctuate compound and compound-complex sentences when applicable.

_____**Use apostrophes** to punctuate contractions, singular possessives, and plural possessives.

_____**Use hyphens, dashes, parentheses, ellipses, and brackets correctly.**

_____**Spell words correctly.**

_____**Use paragraph breaks** to reinforce the organizational structure, including dialogue.

_____**Demonstrate control of grammar and usage** in writing parts of speech, verb forms, verb tenses, subject/verb agreement, pronoun/antecedent agreement, parallel structure, comparative and superlative degrees of adjectives, modifier placement, and homonyms.

_____**Use appropriate format,** according to type of writing, to cite sources (e.g., Chicago, APA, MLA, UPI, any other recognized style manual).

Source: Arizona Department of Education

WORD CHOICE
Word choice reflects the writer's use of specific words and phrases to convey the intended message and employs words appropriate to the audience and purpose.

_____**Use accurate, specific, powerful words and phrases** that effectively convey the intended message.

_____**Use vocabulary that is original, varied, and natural.**

_____**Use words that evoke clear images.**

_____**Use literal and figurative language** intentionally when appropriate.

_____**Use clichés only when appropriate to purpose.**

Finally, there is the Writing Applications category that addresses the question of how your writing serves its potential audience. This category is subdivided into **four types of writing: expository, expressive, functional,** and **persuasive.**

Many of your college research papers will be of the expository type, so pay close attention to the elements in this description.

EXPOSITORY WRITING
Expository writing includes non-fiction writing that describes, explains, or summarizes ideas and content. The writing supports a thesis based on research, observation, and/or experience. Writing is represented by a multi-paragraph essay (e.g., analysis, deduction/induction, problem/solution, extended definition) that:

_____**includes background information** to set up the thesis (hypothesis, essential question), as appropriate

_____**states a thesis** (hypothesis, essential question) with a narrow focus

_____**includes evidence in support of a thesis** (hypothesis, essential question) in the form of details, facts, examples, or reasons

_____**communicates information and ideas from primary and/or secondary sources** accurately and coherently, as appropriate

_____**attributes sources of information** as appropriate

_____**includes a topic sentence for each body paragraph**

_____**includes relevant factors and variables** that need to be considered

_____**includes visual aids** to organize and record information on charts, data tables, maps and graphs, as appropriate

_____**includes an effective conclusion**

Source: Arizona Department of Education

EXPRESSIVE WRITING

Expressive writing includes personal narratives, stories, poetry, songs, and dramatic pieces. Writing may be based on real or imagined events. Writing occurs in a variety of expressive forms (e.g., poetry, fiction, autobiography, narrative, and/or drama). These forms

_____**use voice and style appropriate to audience and purpose**

_____**organize ideas** in writing to ensure coherence, logical progression, and support

_____**employ literary devices** (e.g., irony, conceit, flashback, foreshadowing, symbolism, allusion) to enhance style and voice

---

PERSUASIVE WRITING

Persuasive writing is used for the purpose of influencing the reader. The author presents an issue and expresses an opinion in order to convince an audience to agree with the opinion or to take a particular action. A persuasive composition (e.g. speech, editorial, letter to the editor, public service announcement)

_____**states a position or claim**

_____**presents detailed evidence, examples, and reasoning** to support effective arguments and emotional appeals

_____**attributes sources of information** when appropriate

_____**structures ideas**

_____**acknowledges and refutes opposing arguments**

FUNCTIONAL WRITING

Functional writing provides specific directions or information related to real-world tasks. This includes letters, memos, schedules, directories, signs, manuals, forms, recipes, and technical pieces for specific content areas. Writing is often a work-related document (e.g., resume, application essay) that

_____**presents information purposefully** and succinctly to meet the needs of the intended audience

_____**follows a conventional format**

Source: Arizona Department of Education

A Word About Plagiarism 3

Plagiarism is a form of intellectual property theft. **Plagiarism occurs when a writer "borrows" or "lifts" information or an idea from another source and uses it in his or her work without properly identifying the information, documenting the source, and giving credit to the source.** The writer may be a student, an author, a businessperson, a teacher or any of thousands of other professions where communicating information commonly occurs in written form.

The act of "borrowing" or "lifting" may be intentional. The writer may want to use another writer's information but may not want to ask for permission or pay to use it, or the writer may want to get credit for an idea that is not his or her own. A writer may "lift" someone else's work to meet a deadline or to impress another person. Sometimes, the act of "borrowing" or "lifting" may be accidental: the writer may jot down or copy and paste a sentence or phrase from a source without noting where it came from and then forget that the information hasn't been documented. Sometimes, during research, the writer will find a word or phrase that is particularly memorable, and that word or phrase ends up without attribution in the writer's work because the writer has adopted it as his own. **Either way, lifting or borrowing someone else's information without identifying the information, documenting it, and crediting the source is plagiarism, and plagiarism is a form of theft. It is considered cheating.**

With the advent of computer technology and electronic resources such as databases, websites, and online books for college students, plagiarism has become a major concern. While plagiarism occurs in the workplace just as it does in college, we'll focus on the college setting in this discussion. Because electronic resources make it easy to copy and paste information, and because documenting sources with stylized citations can be a real pain in the backside, some students simply write college papers composed largely of copied-and-pasted information. The student writes an introductory sentence or two, copies and pastes something, changes a few words here and there, changes the order of the sentences in a paragraph, attributes one paragraph of information to a writer that did not write the paragraph but did write articles on similar topics, and voilà! He has a completed paper that he thinks/hopes the instructor will not be able to recognize as plagiarized work.

There are variations on the copy-and-paste method. Some college social organizations and residence units keep former students' research papers on file, allowing new students to "recycle" past students' papers as if they were their own. Siblings may keep their old college papers and hand them down like family heirlooms. Friends at one school may send their papers to friends at other schools.

Some students purchase papers from online companies that sell term and research papers to high school and college students. These companies, often referred to as term paper mills, offer personalized paper-writing services for a fee and sell papers about specific topics that can be purchased with a credit card and downloaded in minutes from the paper mill server to the student. Some companies guarantee that the paper the student is purchasing will be "plagiarism-free" (Paper Masters) or that the purchased paper provides the "ultimate plagiarism fighting solution" (Essayplant.com). Some companies grant the student rights to use the paper or essay as it is delivered. After all, the student paid for the paper or the service that produced the paper; it seems like he should have the right to do with it whatever he wants. Besides, businesses pay for similar sorts of services all the time; what's wrong with purchasing an online paper? Other term paper providers post disclaimers in their "fine print" that state that the paper the student is buying is a study supplement and that the paper should not be used in place of the student's own work (Essayplant.com). Confusion can occur if the student purchasing the paper doesn't read the disclaimer or doesn't understand that a "plagiarism-free" paper purchased from a term paper provider is no longer free of plagiarism if the student claims the work is his or hers when he turns it in to fulfill an assignment. The turned-in purchased paper that was written by someone else is the original writer's work; it is not the work of the student with the credit card. When the student turns in the purchased paper, he is turning in someone else's work, not his own, so the "plagiarism-free" paper becomes a plagiarized paper.

"So," you say, "what's the big deal? Who's going to care if a paper is plagiarized or purchased, or if a few words here and there have been lifted from the Internet? It's not like I robbed a bank."

Colleges and universities care. Professors are very aware of the potential for plagiarism in the college classroom. Colleges and universities subscribe to electronic services that identify plagiarism from previously written student papers as well as from database and Internet resources. Professors and instructors spend hours reading student papers and become sensitive to individual writing styles and nuances that even the student may not realize he or she does. They also communicate with other instructors about evidence of plagiarism in student work. They recognize papers and source material content that they have already read or studied. They can identify the methods students use to lift information from other sources, and they are aware of search engine techniques that can lead them straight to the source of a statement in a student paper. **Never underestimate the tenacity of a professor or instructor who believes she has a plagiarized paper in her hands.**

Businesses and corporations also care about the issue of plagiarism. Employees who claim to be skilled and knowledgeable in a particular field need to be skilled and knowledgeable in that field when they go to work for a company. If an employee plagiarized while he or she was supposedly learning about that field, there's a likelihood that the employee won't know what he or she is supposed to be doing on the job, and that can create problems. There is also the possibility that an employee who has taken credit for someone else's idea or work in a particular field will meet the person who developed the original idea or work. That can be awkward. Or there's the possibility that the employee will be called upon to represent the idea that isn't really his or hers, and the originator of the idea will step up and prove it's his. The notoriety that stems from this sort of situation can destroy a career in a heartbeat. While the workplace has been maligned for its supposed lack of integrity, there are still many companies that value decent, honest, sincere employees with skills they acquired the right way. Workers that plagiarize or have plagiarized are hardly living up to their employers' expectations.

When evidence of plagiarism is found in the college classroom, the instructor or professor may be required to report the occurrence to a supervisor or administrator. Academic policies dictate the consequences for the student who has plagiarized an assignment. These consequences vary from school to school. They typically include a failing grade on the assignment, a failing grade in the course, notation of the plagiarism incident on a student's academic record, expulsion from a course, expulsion from the college or university, or the college's refusal to grant a degree. If the plagiarism is detected after the student has graduated, a school may rescind the degree it granted to the graduate.

To plagiarize or not to plagiarize? It boils down to personal integrity. **When you plagiarize, you put your positive personal image, your integrity, and your honor at risk.** If you want to throw these things away by taking credit for someone else's idea, or by being sloppy or lazy and not identifying someone else's idea, you'll face difficulty in the future when you try to convince a transfer school or an employer that you are honorable enough to be part of their organization. There's also the risk that, in the professional world, you'll meet the person whose work you took the credit for, and that could prove to be at the least rather embarrassing.

Avoiding Plagiarism

How do you avoid plagiarism? The best way to avoid sullying your good name in academia is by being a meticulous researcher and documenting all of your resources and source materials at the time you find them. As you research, copy the date and the documentation/citation information (title, author or editor, publication name, volume, issue, publication date, access date, and page or pages on which your information resides) every time you read an abstract or article in a library database, book, or journal. If you are working at a computer, copy and paste the date and documentation/citation information into a "Source Materials" file; include a few sentences of description of the material you want to use. If you are emailing articles to yourself from a database, copy and paste the documentation/citation information before you email the article; not every database includes the citation information within the emailed article. If you are writing out the information, keep a record of your source materials on index cards or paper; write out the documentation and include a couple of sentences of description about the material, just as if you were tracking the information on an electronic file. **Put quotation marks around every word, phrase, and/or sentence you lift verbatim from the source material, as well as any information you can say you did not know before you read it in the source material.**

Taking notes of citations is one instance where the "copy-and-paste" method is acceptable.

Information that is common knowledge does not have to be cited in the text of a paper. Little-known facts, as well as interpretations and paraphrases of little-known facts, do need to be cited. Err on the side of caution when you use facts that may or may not be common knowledge. Cite them whenever you aren't sure that at least three people in your immediate vicinity would know the information. For example, college literature students commonly know that Harper Lee wrote the novel titled *To Kill a Mockingbird*. When you use this information in a college research paper, such as it is presented in this sentence – "Harper Lee was the author of the novel titled *To Kill a Mockingbird*" – the fact does not have to be cited. What is probably not common knowledge is the observation by author Charles J. Shields in his book, *Mockingbird: A Portrait of Harper Lee,* that Harper Lee as a child spied on her neighbor, Truman, from a tree house located in a chinaberry tree. The original information on page 34 of Shields's book states: "Next to the wall grew a twin-trunk chinaberry tree supporting a tree house. From this outpost, Nelle could spy on Truman ambling among the lilacs and azaleas." If you use this information, even as a paraphrased statement, you will need to provide a citation in the text, as indicated here:

> In *Mockingbird,* a biography of Nelle Harper Lee, it is noted that Harper Lee spent part of her childhood spying on the next-door neighbor boy from a tree house in her family's yard (Shields 34). The boy would grow up to be Truman Capote; the two would eventually become good friends.

You will also need to provide a complete citation in your paper's bibliography, such as the citation presented here in MLA style:

> Shields, Charles J. *Mockingbird: A Portrait of Harper Lee.* New York: Henry Holt and Company, 2006.

If you aren't sure whether you should cite something because you aren't sure whether the fact is common knowledge, it's wiser to cite it both in the text and as a bibliographic citation.

You probably have other questions about documenting source materials, citations, and plagiarism. Style guides, which will be discussed in greater detail in chapters 12 and 21, are an excellent source of information about how to document source materials and write citations. Online instruction developed by the writing centers at Indiana University *(www.indiana.edu/~wts/pamphlets/plagiarism.shtml)* and Purdue University *(http://owl.english.purdue.edu)* offers excellent information about ways to avoid plagiarism. Some of the plagiarism issues addressed by the Georgetown University Honor Council *(http://gervaseprograms.georgetown.edu/honor/system/53377.html)* are also addressed here, along with a few of the more common questions and comments I heard from my students:

Where I grew up it is considered a compliment to borrow and use someone else's words without giving them credit for their work.

While it is true that some cultures do not consider it an offense to use another person's words without identifying the words and documenting the source, it is important for you to recognize and honor the expectations and policies where you are attending school. If the school you attend has no academic or disciplinary policies regarding plagiarism, cheating, academic integrity, or academic dishonesty, then you should consider yourself lucky. College will be easy. You will be able to copy and paste until your fingerprints wear off. If, on the other hand, the school you attend has academic or disciplinary policies regarding academic dishonesty, cheating, plagiarism, or academic integrity, you would be wise to read and honor the policies, and avoid taking a risk that could bring your academic career to an abrupt and disappointing end.

It's not plagiarism if I take something off the Internet or off the news and use it in my paper because that stuff is public information. I'm not stealing it.

Oh, but you are. If you use information or ideas from any source, including the Internet or the news, and fail to identify the information or idea and document the source, you are in essence stealing intellectual property. People borrow and lift other people's original materials all the time on the Internet because it seems like one big grab bag of information, without restrictions or rules. The truth is, each **original** photo, story, article, idea, game, and advertisement on the Internet was created by someone who owns the copyright or trademark to the original work. The term *public domain* refers to property not controlled by anyone; news articles and Internet content are controlled by the people and companies that created them.

Maybe it will help to look at it this way: If you post on the Internet a poem that you wrote, it is still your poem; you own the copyright to it and control it because you are the one that wrote it. By posting it on the Internet, you have put your copyrighted work on display. Now, though, everybody in the world can copy and paste your poem and call it their own. When Sam Smith copies and pastes your poem, slaps his name on it, posts it on his website as an original work by Sam Smith and fails to give you credit for creating the work in the first place, he has committed plagiarism/intellectual property theft. You as the original owner have been wronged by Sam Smith's thievery and can seek restitution. If you can prove that you are the creator of the poem, then you have proven that Sam Smith committed plagiarism. The same holds true for information broadcast on the news. A news story read by a news anchor on a copyrighted news broadcast was produced for the news agency that employs both the anchor and the reporter who wrote the story. Because the broadcast was copyrighted, the rights to the news story belong to the news agency that employs the anchor and the reporter. Just because you don't have to pay someone to access information does not mean it's in the public domain and free for the taking.

It's so much easier and faster to copy and paste stuff than it is to rewrite it.

It's probably easier to shoplift, too, than it is to work to earn the money to buy clothes. That doesn't make it right. When you take shortcuts that can have negative consequences on your future, you are putting yourself at risk for the sake of laziness, convenience, indifference, or any of several other not-so-flattering reasons. Oh, and did I mention that you don't learn much if all you do is move text from one place to another? Planning your schedule so that you have enough time to complete a writing assignment will help you stay out of the situations were copying and pasting become a temptation. If you are in a crunch for time, talk to your professor or instructor about alternate arrangements *before* the due date of your assignment.

The way it's written in the source material sounds so much better than I can write it.

That may be true, but part of the learning process involves pushing yourself beyond the limits of your comfort zone and ability level to develop and improve your skills. Good writing doesn't just happen to you as a writer; you have to work at it and develop good writing skills. When you read something that is well written and easy to understand, and you take the time to analyze why it is well written and easy to understand, there is potential for you to learn how to write well-written and easy-to-understand things. As you practice writing by writing, you become more knowledgeable about the purpose of writing and about word choice, organization of ideas, structure, fluency, grammar, spelling, punctuation, and all the other elements that constitute writing. As you become more knowledgeable about the elements of writing, you become more comfortable with ways to use them effectively. As you become more comfortable with the act of writing, your command over the language becomes more powerful. Your sentences and your style become clearer, and your message becomes more interesting. You look at a sentence in the source material and you say to yourself, "I can say that better in my own words," and kaboom! Pretty soon, your writing sounds every bit as wonderful and profound as the writing of the author of the source material.

What if someone else in my class or project group says something I want to use in my paper? Do I credit him or her for the idea? What if it's not an original idea, but she's just repeating something she read or heard? How far back do I have to research something to be sure it's an original idea?

Identifying others' information and ideas and giving them credit for their work are important activities within the academic community. If you are working with a group of students and someone makes the remark, "I have this theory about this topic," you should encourage the student to elaborate if you believe it's a well-founded theory or idea that you want to use in your paper. You should also ask if the idea is hers or his, or whether it belongs to someone else. If the student can claim ownership of the theory or idea, you should credit the student as the source of the material within the text of your paper and in your bibliography. If the student says, "Aw, it's just something I read somewhere," and you believe you can't live without the information, then it's up to you to research the idea and try to find its origin. Once you find it, you can cite the source within the text of your paper and in the bibliography.

Documenting sources and writing citations in the correct style or format is a huge pain in the patootie. What's the payoff?

Documenting your sources and learning to write citations are parts of the college experience. Knowing what you've read so that you can develop an argument or opinion for a paper will help you to build your knowledge base. Writing citations in the correct style or format will help you to improve your organization skills. Documentation may seem like a subtle form of torture, but when you document sources and write citations, you are demonstrating to your professors that you know how to follow the rules in an academic environment.

How do I quote something from an original text if I don't want to use all of it because there are a lot of extra words and phrases that seem unnecessary?

It is important to retain the idea and the intent of a text when you use it as a resource, regardless of whether you are quoting it verbatim or paraphrasing it. If the text is long and you can take from it, without altering the meaning, a single phrase or sentence instead of using the entire quote, take the single phrase or sentence and put it in quotation marks. If you must use the whole text, then consider using it as a block quote if the text occupies more than four lines of space in your paper. If the passage has phrases that are not critical to the idea and intent of the author and the overall message, these phrases can be removed and replaced with ellipsis marks (...) to indicate that text is missing. Here are four different ways to use a portion of a longer text:

ORIGINAL TEXT FROM PAGE 7 OF AN ARTICLE BY SUSAN FERGUSON: It is never enough for Victor to understand just one means to an end. Throughout the entire novel *Cellophane,* it is apparent that he has to learn and understand everything that lies on parallel paths – paper factories in the city versus those in the jungle, brown paper versus cellophane, the methods of the *curandero* versus those of the priest, the intimacy of his lovers versus that of his wife. Knowledge, Victor implies, occurs as a result of truth. Truth creates transparency. Transparency creates understanding and the capacity to move forward.

1) DIRECT QUOTE-SINGLE SENTENCE

Victor, the protagonist of *Cellophane,* spends his life studying and learning about the nature of relationships between objects and forces in his world. "Knowledge, Victor implies, occurs as a result of truth" (Ferguson 7). The more he learns, the more he is empowered to make progress in his life.

2) BLOCK QUOTE WITH ELLIPSES

Victor, the protagonist of *Cellophane,* devotes his life to studying and learning because he is motivated by the promise of knowledge:

> It is never enough for Victor to understand just one means to an end... He has to learn and understand everything that lies on parallel paths.... Knowledge, Victor implies, occurs as a result of truth. Truth creates transparency. Transparency creates understanding and the capacity to move forward in a positive way (Ferguson 7).

3) BLOCK QUOTE

Victor, the protagonist of *Cellophane,* devotes his life to studying and learning because he is motivated by the promise of knowledge:

> It is never enough for Victor to understand just one means to an end. Throughout the entire novel, it is apparent that he has to learn and understand everything that lies on parallel paths – paper factories in the city versus those in the jungle, brown paper versus cellophane, the methods of the *curandero* versus those of the priest, the intimacy of his lovers versus that of his wife. Knowledge, Victor implies, occurs as a result of truth. Truth creates transparency. Transparency creates understanding and the capacity to move forward in a positive way (Ferguson 7).

4) PARAPHRASE

Ferguson states in the journal article that Victor, the protagonist of *Cellophane,* devotes his life to studying and learning because he believes that knowing the truth is the best way to make progress.

How do I paraphrase something without using the same words that the original author did?

Paraphrasing is an interpretation and restatement of an original text. While you may need to use some of the key words from the original text in order to reinforce your connection with the topic and the view of the author, you are wiser to use fewer and newer words than there were in the original text and to be succinct in your paraphrase so that your fresh interpretation is clearly evident. Take a look at this example, where the key words are in bold type:

ORIGINAL TEXT: **Natural environments** should be allowed to undergo **natural processes** without interference from **civilization.** However, it appears that civilization is engaged in some sort of **meddlesome control over nature and the wilderness** in the **United States** to the extent that what was once important as a **symbol of freedom** has now become important as a **symbol of freedom in captivity.**

WEAK PARAPHRASE: The processes of nature should happen without civilization's interference. Nonetheless, civilization in the United States controls so much of nature that it is now thought of as a wild thing in a cage.

Sounds too much like the style of the original text.

STRONG PARAPHRASE: The American wilderness is losing its identity as an uncivilized place due to the pressures exerted by people and modern development.

Short, succinct sentence uses only a few key words to restate the original idea.

As you start doing research for the various papers you write, you may hear from others in your classes that plagiarism isn't a big deal, that nobody ever gets caught, that copying-and-pasting saves time and energy, that papers sound better if you use other people's stuff. Plagiarism is a big deal, people do get caught, saving time and energy is not the reason you enrolled in college, and plagiarized papers often sound like gibberish. If you remember nothing else from your comp class experience, remember this: Plagiarism is a form of intellectual property theft. When you plagiarize, you are making the assumption that the person from whom you are stealing is smarter than you. Look around at the people that populate your world, the stuff you read online, and the conversations you overhear when you're out and about. Do you really want to make that assumption?

How Do You Learn? **4**

In the 1980s psychologist and education professor Howard Gardner proposed the theory of multiple intelligences. This theory addresses the ways a person gathers information and processes it in order to learn it. Gardner's theory reinforced teachers' observations about their students' learning experiences and created a framework for teaching in the modern education system.

Gardner's theory supports the idea that intelligence develops and functions uniquely in individuals. It is not a "thing" like blue eyes or red hair that is passed down from one generation to the next, and it is not something that can be improved or enhanced by a single academic act. Rather, the theory of multiple intelligences puts forth the idea that an individual's ability to process information in order to solve problems and accomplish goals – the basic tenet of learning – is rooted in the individual's physical and psychological makeup. Hence, a person who is a "visual learner" will learn more readily by viewing a concept presented in charts and images than he will learn by listening to someone explain the concept in words. A person who "learns by doing" is more likely to understand how to build a bookshelf by holding the pieces in his hands and putting them together than he is by reading and interpreting the printed instructions. Gardner's initial theory of multiple intelligences included seven mechanisms:

- Linguistic/verbal intelligence
- Logical/mathematical intelligence
- Musical/rhythmic intelligence
- Bodily/kinetic intelligence
- Visual/spatial intelligence
- Interpersonal intelligence
- Intrapersonal intelligence

Gardner also indicated that more than one type of intelligence could function at the same time to help a person process information. For example, a person who has a job in retail sales or marketing may have to call on his or her linguistic intelligence to memorize pricing information and his or her visual/spatial intelligence in order to understand which items correlate to the various prices.

As a student of English composition, you will be faced with challenges and tasks to think critically, interpret, and analyze ideas and information; document data; write papers; construct presentations; and meet assignment deadlines and expectations. If we use Gardner's theory as a model, we can safely state that these challenges and tasks are problems you will need to solve and goals you will need to accomplish in order to learn English composition. If you have at the outset a solid understanding of how you learn, you will be better able to develop the skills you need. You will learn more efficiently and effectively if you understand how to utilize your mind and body to best advantage.

Presented in this self-quiz are brief explanations of the different types of intelligences identified in Gardner's theory. As you read, think about learning experiences you have had during the past year. Think of the activities you undertook that helped you to learn a new concept or new information. Make a note of significant learning experiences beneath the description that most directly applies. When you think about the way you have learned since you were a child, do any obvious learning patterns emerge? If so, what are they? Please take a few minutes to answer the questions at the end of the list. Your new awareness of your own intelligences will help you as you continue to study.

Self-Quiz:
How Do You Learn?

As you read through the description of each intelligence, ask yourself whether you utilize the intelligence as you learn. You may use more than one type of intelligence. Jot down any recollections you may have about learning experiences relating to a specific type of intelligence.

LINGUISTIC/VERBAL INTELLIGENCE – sensitivity to spoken and written language. A person who utilizes this form of intelligence uses language effectively, uses language to remember information, learns other languages with relative ease, and uses language to accomplish tasks and goals.

_____

_____

_____

_____

LOGICAL/MATHEMATICAL INTELLIGENCE – sensitivity to mathematical processes, logical analysis, and interpretation. A person with logical/mathematical intelligence can detect patterns, use deductive reasoning, and relate to logical scientific and mathematical experiences.

_____

_____

_____

_____

MUSICAL/RHYTHMIC INTELLIGENCE – sensitivity to rhythmic patterns. A person with musical intelligence can detect musical rhythms, tones, and pitches, and compose and perform the rhythms with ease.

_____

_____

_____

_____

BODILY/KINETIC INTELLIGENCE – sensitivity to the use of the body or its parts to solve problems and accomplish tasks. This bodily activity is tied directly to the mind's ability to co-ordinate movement related to the task.

_____

_____

_____

_____

VISUAL/SPATIAL INTELLIGENCE – skill relating to the awareness of patterns in shapes, dimensions, and sizes. This type of intelligence recognizes and utilizes shapes and forms to solve problems and accomplish tasks.

_____

_____

_____

_____

INTERPERSONAL INTELLIGENCE – sensitivity to the behaviors, intentions, motivations, and goals of others as a way to solve problems and accomplish tasks. A person who utilizes interpersonal intelligence identifies others' actions in order to coordinate or manage the actions.

_____

_____

_____

_____

INTRAPERSONAL INTELLIGENCE – an introspective sensitivity toward one's own emotions, thoughts, and behaviors in an effort to understand the self.

_____

_____

_____

_____

_____

_____

List some of the learning experiences you have had during the past year. How was information presented to you in those situations that made it possible for you to understand the concept or information?

_____

_____

_____

_____

_____

_____

Can you think of other experiences in which you learned in a unique way?

_____

_____

_____

_____

As you reviewed the items in this self-quiz, did you determine which type(s) of intelligence applies(y) to you? Which? Why?

_____

_____

_____

_____

_____

_____

The Power of Critical Thinking **5**

emember when you were a little kid and your parents told you with a stern voice and grim expression not to touch the stove because it was hot and you could burn yourself? Remember how you believed them, even though you weren't exactly sure what a "stove" was and what "hot" or "burn" meant…. Then, one day, you were in the kitchen and Mom or Dad turned away for just a second and you put your finger on what they kept calling the stove and discovered that not only was the stove hot but it did indeed burn your finger, which hurt a lot. You yelled "Hot!" and cried, and when your parents said, "See, we told you so," you at last understood that you shouldn't touch the stove because the consequences weren't good, and after that, you avoided touching the stove at all. That was probably your first experience with critical thinking. The situation has all the hallmarks of critical thinking:

1) You received information: Your parents told you not to touch the stove because it was "hot."

2) You interpreted information: The tone of your parents' voice and the expression on their faces made touching the stove sound and look serious and scary.

3) You analyzed information: The tone of your parents' voice and their facial expression, combined with their emphasis of the word "hot," sounded like other warnings they gave you about dangerous things so that must mean there was some danger or risk involved in touching the stove.

4) You evaluated information: Your parents' tone and facial expression made touching the stove sound like a serious and scary act. However, you could not be sure what the danger was until you actually put your finger on the stove to determine what a "hot" stove felt like and what kind of consequence there was in getting a "burn" from touching a "hot" stove.

5) You inferred from the information you interpreted, analyzed, and evaluated: The burning sensation in your finger told you that your parents were correct, that touching the stove was a dangerous, serious, scary (and now painful) thing to do.

6) You expressed or explained your reasoning: Yelling "Hot!" and crying and saying "I burned my finger because the stove was hot!" are ways to express reaction and understanding that your parents were correct when they implied that touching the stove was a dangerous, serious, scary thing to do. Your parents' acknowledgement of your expressions of pain and sadness served as a reinforcement of the overarching message.

7) You self-regulated your reasoning: By staying away from the stove or putting your hand

near it but not on it to detect its temperature on several occasions, you reinforced the concept you just learned – that you shouldn't touch a "hot" stove because it is dangerous and can cause pain.

Critical thinking is the crux of learning. From our simple example about the hot stove to the more complex issues of deciding who to vote for or what clothing to buy, you use some if not all of the steps involved in critical thinking every day of your life. When you look for new friends, you use critical thinking to evaluate others' behavior and decide whether it matches your expectations. When you apply for a job, you use critical thinking to determine which jobs are best suited to your personality, interests, and skills. When you write a college paper, you call on your critical thinking skills to identify your thesis or claim and then find and present evidence to support it.

Critical thinking helps us to solve problems and accomplish goals by helping us to understand the reality or value of the things we experience and observe in our lives. It helps us to appreciate the significance of our experiences and observations by allowing us to interpret, analyze, and evaluate the information and ideas we receive from other sources and put them into perspective alongside information and ideas we already possess. When we think critically, we are utilizing specific pathways of reasoning in our brain to receive, interpret, analyze, and evaluate information and ideas; to express our understanding of the information and ideas; and to reinforce our new understanding by revisiting the process of analysis and reviewing our conclusions against any new information and ideas we receive.

The process of critical thinking goes hand in hand with creative thinking. Many books and articles have been written about the correlation between critical thinking and creative thought. In *A Guide for Educators to Critical Thinking Competency Standards,* authors Richard Paul and Linda Elder state that critical and creative thought are interrelated:

> Creativity masters a process of making or producing; criticality, a process of assessing or judging. The mind when thinking well must simultaneously both produce and assess, both generate and judge, the products it constructs. Sound thinking requires both imagination and intellectual discipline…. (Paul and Elder 13)

When we learn something – when we learn anything – our brain processes the information through a series of steps. Paul and Elder describe the process as a "series of mental acts" as they discuss learning a subject such as English or mathematics:

> To learn the key concepts in a discipline, we must construct them in our minds by a series of mental acts. We must construct them as an ordered system of relationships. We must construct both foundations and the concepts derivative of those foundations. Each moment of that creation requires discernment and judgment. There is no way to implant, transfer, or inject the system in the mind of another person in prefabricated form. It cannot be put on a mental compact disk and downloaded into the mind without an intellectual struggle. Critical judgment is essential to all acts of construction; and all acts of construction are open to critical assessment. We create and assess; we assess what we create; we assess as we create. In other words, at one and the same time, we think critically and creatively. (Paul and Elder 13)

Scholar and philosopher Peter Facione has written a superb essay about critical thinking.

As you read the essay, take particular note of the elements in bold lettering and the graphics featuring quotes and illustrations that are presented throughout the essay. These elements are key to your recognition and understanding of the concepts of critical thinking. Apply each concept to a recent experience in your life and identify ways you utilized the concept to help solve a problem or accomplish a goal. Pay attention to the tone, style, sentence structure, word choice, and grammar of Facione's essay. At the end of the essay are a few questions to help you to identify the key points and the overall message of Facione's writing. As you answer the questions, consider how your reading of the essay has helped you to understand the concept of critical thinking.

Critical Thinking: What It Is and Why It Counts

By Peter A. Facione

George Carlin worked "critical thinking" into one of his monologue rants on the perils of trusting our lives and fortunes to the decision-making of a gullible, uninformed, and unreflective citizenry. The argument that higher education – while surely both – is more of a public good than a private good is beginning to be recognized. Is it not a wiser social policy to invest in the education of the future workforce, rather than to suffer the financial loses and endure the fiscal and social burdens associated with economic weakness, public health problems, crime, and avoidable poverty?

Teach people to make good decisions and you equip them to improve their own futures and become contributing members of society, rather than burdens on society. Becoming educated and practicing good judgment does not absolutely guarantee a life of happiness, virtue, or economic success, but it surely offers a better chance at those things. And it is clearly better than enduring the consequences of making bad decisions and better than burdening friends, family, and all the rest of us with the unwanted and avoidable consequences of those poor choices.

Defining Critical Thinking

Yes, surely we have all heard business executives, policy makers, civic leaders, and educators talking about critical thinking. At times we found ourselves wondering exactly what critical thinking was and why is it considered so useful and important. This essay takes a deeper look at these questions.

But, rather than beginning with an abstract definition – as if critical thinking were about memorization, which is not the case – give this thought experiment a try: Imagine you have been invited to a movie by a friend. But it's not a movie you want to see. So, your friend asks you why. You give your honest reason. The movie offends your sense of decency. Your friend asks you to clarify your reason by explaining what bothers you about the film. You reply that it is not the language used or the sexuality portrayed, but you find the violence in the film offensive.

Sure, that should be a good enough answer. But suppose your friend, perhaps being a bit philosophically inclined or simply curious or argumentative, pursues the matter further by asking you to define what you mean by "offensive violence."

Take a minute and give it a try. How would you define "offensive violence" as it applies to movies? Can you write a characterization that captures what this commonly used concept contains? Take care, though; we would not want to make the definition so broad that all movie violence would be automatically "offensive." And check to be sure your way of defining "offensive violence" fits with how the rest of the people who know and use English would understand the term. Otherwise they will not be able to understand what you mean when you use that expression.

Did you come up with a definition that works? How do you know? What you just did with the expression "offensive violence" is very much the same as what had to be done with the expression "critical thinking." At one level we all know what "critical thinking" means — it means good thinking, almost the opposite of illogical, irrational thinking. But when we test our understanding further, we run into questions. For example, is critical thinking the same as creative thinking? Are they different, or is one part of the other? How do critical thinking and native intelligence or scholastic aptitude relate? Does critical thinking focus on the subject matter or content that you know or on the process you use when you reason about that content?

It might not hurt at all if you formed some tentative preliminary ideas about the questions we just raised. We humans learn better when we stop frequently to reflect, rather than just plowing from the top of the page to the bottom without coming up for air.

Fine. So how would you propose we go about defining "critical thinking"? You do not really want a definition plopped on the page for you to memorize, do you? That would be silly, almost counterproductive. The goal here is to help you sharpen your critical thinking skills and cultivate your critical thinking spirit. While memorization definitely has many valuable uses, fostering critical thinking is not among them. So, let's look back at what you might have done to define "offensive violence" and see if we can learn from you. Did you think of some scenes in movies that were offensively violent, and did you contrast them with other scenes that were either not violent or not offensively violent? If you did, good. That is one (but not the only) way to approach the problem. Technically it is called *finding paradigm cases*. Happily, like many things in life, you do not have to know its name to do it well.

Back to critical thinking. What might be some paradigm cases? How about the adroit and clever questioning of Socrates? Or, what about police detectives, crime scene analysts, or trial lawyers, as portrayed in TV dramas and movies? What about people working together to solve a problem? How about someone who is good at listening to all sides of a dispute, considering all the facts, and then deciding what is relevant and what is not, and then rendering a thoughtful judgment? And maybe too, someone who is able to summarize complex ideas clearly with fairness to all sides, or a person who can come up with the most coherent and justifiable explanation of what a passage of written material means? Or the person who can readily devise sensible alternatives to explore, but who does not become defensive about abandoning them if they do not work? And also the person who can explain exactly how a particular conclusion was reached, or why certain criteria apply?

> *How has CT changed my life? Critical thinking is my life; it's my philosophy of life. It's how I define myself... I'm an educator because I think these ideas have meaning. I'm convinced that what we believe in has to be able to stand the test of evaluation.*
> *— John Chaffee, author of* Critical Thinking[1]

An international group of experts was asked to try to form a consensus about the meaning of critical thinking. One of the first things they did was to ask themselves the question: Who are the best critical thinkers we know and what is it about them that leads us to consider them the best? So, who are the best critical thinkers you know? Why do you think they are good critical thinkers? Can you draw from those examples a description that is more abstract? For example, consider effective trial lawyers; apart from how they conduct their personal lives or whether their client is really guilty or innocent, just look at how the lawyers develop their cases in court. They use reasons to try to convince the judge and jury of their client's claim to guilt or innocence. They offer evidence and evaluate the significance of the evidence presented by the opposition lawyers. They interpret testimony. They analyze and evaluate the arguments advanced by the other side.

Now, consider the example of a team of people trying to solve a problem. The team members, unlike the courtroom's adversarial situation, try to collaborate. The members of an effective team do not compete against each other. They work in concert, like colleagues, for the common goal. Unless they solve the problem, none of them has won. When they find the way to solve the problem, they all have won. So, from analyzing just two examples we can generalize something very important: *critical thinking* is thinking that has a purpose (proving a point, interpreting what something means, solving a problem), but critical thinking can be a collaborative, noncompetitive endeavor. And, by the way, even lawyers collaborate. They can work together on a common defense or a joint prosecution, and they can also cooperate with each other to get at the truth so that justice is done.

We will come to a more precise definition of critical thinking soon enough. But first, there is something else we can learn from paradigm examples. When you were thinking about "offensive violence," did you come up with any examples that were tough to classify? Borderline cases, as it were — an example that one person might consider offensive but another might reasonably regard as non-offensive. Yes, well, so did we. This is going to happen with all abstract concepts.

It happens with the concept of critical thinking as well. There are people of whom we would say: on certain occasions this person is a good thinker – clear, logical, thoughtful, attentive to the facts, open to alternatives. But wow, at other times, look out! When you get this person on such-and-such a topic, well, it is all over then. You have pushed some kind of button and the person does not want to hear what anybody else has to say. The person's mind is made up ahead of time. New facts are pushed aside. No other point of view is tolerated.

Do you know any people that might fit that general description?

Good. What can we learn about critical thinking from such a case? Maybe more than we can learn from just looking at the easy cases. When a case is on the borderline, it forces us to make important distinctions. It confronts us and demands a decision: In or Out! And not just that, but why? So, our friend who is fair-minded about some things but close-minded about others, what to do? Let's take the parts we approve of because they seem to us to contribute to acting rationally and logically and include those in the concept of critical thinking, and let's take the parts that work against reason, that close the mind to the possibility of new and relevant information, that blindly deny even the possibility that the other side might have merit, and call those parts poor, counterproductive, or uncritical thinking.

Now, formulate a list of cases — people that are clearly good critical thinkers and clearly poor critical thinkers and some who are on the borderline. Considering all those cases, what is it about them that led you to decide which were which? Suggestion: What can the good critical thinkers do (what mental abilities do they have) that the poor critical thinkers have trouble doing? What attitudes or approaches do the good critical thinkers habitually seem to exhibit which the poor critical thinkers seem not to possess?

Very few really seek knowledge in this world. Mortal or immortal, few really ask. On the contrary, they try to wring from the unknown the answers they have already shaped in their own minds – justification, explanations, forms of consolation without which they can't go on. To really ask is to open the door to the whirlwind. The answer may annihilate the question and the questioner.

– Spoken by the Vampire Marius in Ann Rice's book The Vampire Lestat

Critical Thinking Skills

We suggested you look for a list of mental abilities and attitudes or habits that experts, when faced with the same problem you are working on, refer to as *cognitive skills* and *dispositions*. As to the cognitive skills, here is what the experts include as being at the very core of critical thinking: **interpretation, analysis, evaluation, inference, explanation, and self-regulation.** (We will get to the dispositions in just a second.) Did any of these words or ideas come up when you tried to characterize the cognitive skills — mental abilities — involved in critical thinking?

Quoting from the consensus statement of the national panel of experts: **interpretation** is "to comprehend and express the meaning or significance of a wide variety of experiences, situations, data, events, judgments, conventions, beliefs, rules, procedures, or criteria."[2]

Interpretation includes the sub-skills of categorization, decoding significance, and clarifying meaning. Can you think of examples of interpretation? How about recognizing a problem and describing it without bias? How about reading a person's intentions in the expression on her face; distinguishing a main idea from subordinate ideas in a text; constructing a tentative categorization or way of organizing something you are studying; paraphrasing someone's ideas in your own words; or, clarifying what a sign, chart or graph means? What about identifying an author's purpose, theme, or point of view? How about what you did above when you clarified what "offensive violence" meant?

You will use these sub-skills a great deal during the prewriting stage of an essay.

CORE CRITICAL THINKING SKILLS

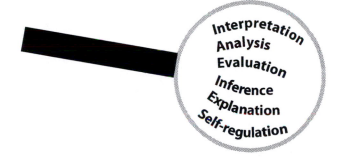

Figure 2 By applying each of the six core critical thinking skills, a person facing a problem can find a thoughtful solution.

Again from the experts: **analysis** is "to identify the intended and actual inferential relationships among statements, questions, concepts, descriptions, or other forms of representation intended to express belief, judgment, experiences, reasons, information, or opinions." **The experts include examining ideas, detecting arguments, and analyzing arguments as sub-skills of analysis.** Again, can you come up with some examples of analysis? What about identifying the similarities and differences between two approaches to the solution of a given problem? What about picking out the main claim made in a newspaper editorial and tracing back the various reasons the editor offers in support of that claim? Or, what about identifying unstated assumptions; constructing a way to represent a main conclusion and the various reasons given to support or criticize it; sketching the relationship of sentences or paragraphs to each other and to the main purpose of the passage? What about graphically organizing this essay, in your own way, knowing that its purpose is to give a preliminary idea about what critical thinking means?

These sub-skills will come in handy during the research and thesis development stages of essay writing.

The experts define **evaluation** as meaning "to assess the credibility of statements or other representations which are accounts or descriptions of a person's perception, experience, situation, judgment, belief, or opinion; and to assess the logical strength of the actual or intended inferential relationships among statements, descriptions, questions or other forms of representation." Your examples? How about judging an author's or speaker's credibility, comparing the strengths and weaknesses of alternative interpretations, determining the credibility of a source of information, judging if two statements contradict each other, or judging if the evidence at hand supports the conclusion being drawn? Among the examples the experts propose are these: "**recognizing the factors** which make a person a credible witness regarding a given event or a credible authority with regard to a given topic," "**judging** if **an argument's conclusion** follows either with certainty or with a high level of confidence from its premises," "judging the logical strength of arguments based on hypothetical situations," "judging if a given argument is relevant or applicable or has implications for the situation at hand."

As you identify the points you want to use to make your own essays convincing, you will need these skills to evaluate your source materials.

Do the people you regard as good critical thinkers have the three cognitive skills described so far? Are they good at interpretation, analysis, and evaluation? And your examples of poor critical thinkers – are they lacking in these cognitive skills? All, or just some? What about the next three?

To the experts **inference** means "to identify and secure elements needed to draw reasonable conclusions; to form conjectures and hypotheses; to consider relevant information and to educe the consequences flowing from data, statements, principles, evidence, judgments, beliefs, opinions, concepts, descriptions, questions, or other forms of representation." **As sub-skills of inference the experts list querying evidence, conjecturing alternatives, and drawing conclusions.** Can you think of some examples of inference? You might suggest things like seeing the implications of the position someone is advocating, or drawing out or constructing meaning from the elements in a reading. You may suggest that predicting what will happen next is based on what is known about the forces at work in a given situation, or formulate a synthesis of related ideas into a coherent perspective. How about this: after judging that it would be useful to you to resolve a given uncertainty, you should develop a workable plan to gather that information. Or, when faced with a problem, developing a set of options for addressing it. What about conducting a controlled experiment scientifically and applying the proper statistical methods to attempt to confirm or disconfirm an empirical hypothesis?

These sub-skills will help you to recognize the rhetorical appeals you need to use in your essay to persuade your audience.

Beyond being able to interpret, analyze, evaluate, and infer, good critical thinkers can do two more things. They can explain what they think and how they arrived at that judgment. And they can apply their powers of critical thinking to themselves and improve on their previous opinions. These two skills are called "explanation" and "self-regulation."

The experts define **explanation** as being able to present in a cogent and coherent way the results of one's reasoning. This means to be able to give someone a full look at the big picture: both "to state and to justify that reasoning in terms of the evidential, conceptual, methodological, criteriological, and contextual considerations upon which one's results were based; and to present one's reasoning in the form of cogent arguments." **The sub-skills under explanation are**

These sub-skills will be valuable as you draft your essay and revise it.

- **describing methods and results**
- **justifying procedures**
- **proposing and defending with good reasons one's causal and conceptual explanations of events or points of view**
- **presenting full and well-reasoned arguments in the context of seeking the best understandings possible.**

Here are some examples of explanation:

- to construct a chart which organizes one's findings
- to write down for future reference your current thinking on some important and complex matter to cite the standards and contextual factors used to judge the quality of an interpretation of a text
- to state research results and describe the methods and criteria used to achieve those results
- to appeal to established criteria as a way of showing the reasonableness of a given judgment
- to design a graphic display which accurately represents the subordinate and super-ordinate relationship among concepts or ideas
- to site the evidence that led you to accept or reject an author's position on an issue
- to list the factors that were considered in assigning a final course grade.

Maybe the most remarkable cognitive skill of all, however, is this next one. This one is remarkable because it allows good critical thinkers to improve their own thinking. In a sense this is critical thinking applied to itself. Because of that some people want to call this "metacognition," meaning it raises thinking to another level. But "another level" really does not fully capture it, because at that next level up what self-regulation does is look back at all the dimensions of critical thinking and double-check itself. **Self-regulation** is like a recursive function in mathematical terms, which means it can apply to everything, including itself. You can monitor and correct an interpretation you offered. You can examine and correct an inference you have drawn. You can review and reformulate one of your own explanations. You can even examine and correct your ability to examine and correct yourself! How? It is as simple as stepping back and saying to yourself, "How am I doing? Have I missed anything important? Let me double-check before I go further."

The experts define **self-regulation** to mean "self-consciously to monitor one's cognitive activities, the elements used in those activities, and the results educed, particularly by applying skills in analysis, and evaluation to one's own inferential judgments with a view toward questioning, confirming, validating, or correcting either one's reasoning or one's results." **The two sub-skills here are self-examination and self-correction.** Examples? Easy —

As you edit and revise your essay, you will use these skills to interpret, analyze, and evaluate your own writing.

- to examine your views on a controversial issue with sensitivity to the possible influences of your personal biases or self-interest
- to check yourself when listening to a speaker to be sure you are understanding what the person is really saying without introducing your own ideas
- to monitor how well you seem to be understanding or comprehending what you are reading or experiencing
- to remind yourself to separate your personal opinions and assumptions from those of the author of a passage or text
- to double-check yourself by recalculating the figures
- to vary your reading speed and method mindful of the type of material and your purpose for reading
- to reconsider your interpretation or judgment in view of further analysis of the facts of the case
- to revise your answers in view of the errors you discovered in your work
- to change your conclusion in view of the realization that you had misjudged the importance of certain factors when coming to your earlier decision.

The Delphi Method

The panel of experts we keep referring to included forty-six men and women from throughout the United States and Canada. They represented many different scholarly disciplines in the humanities, sciences, social sciences, and education. They participated in a research project that lasted two years and was conducted on behalf of the American Philosophical Association. Their work was published under the title *Critical Thinking: A Statement of Expert Consensus for Purposes of Educational Assessment and Instruction.* (The California Academic Press, Millbrae, CA, 1990). The executive summary of that report is available at *www.insightassessment.com/articles.html.*

You might be wondering how such a large group of people could collaborate on this project over that long a period of time and at those distances and still come to consensus. Good question. Remember, we're talking the days before e-mail. Not only did the group have to rely on snail mail during their two-year collaboration; they also relied on a method of interaction, known as the Delphi Method, which was developed precisely to enable experts to think effectively about something over large spans of distance and time. In the Delphi Method a central investigator organizes the group and feeds them an initial question. [In this case it had to do with how college-level critical thinking should be defined so that people teaching at that level would know which skills and dispositions to cultivate in their students.] The central investigator receives all responses, summarizes them, and transmits them back to all the panelists for reactions, replies, and additional questions.

Wait a minute! These are all well-known experts, so what do you do if people disagree? And what about the possible influence of a big-name person? Good points. First, the central investigator takes precautions to remove names so that the panelists are not told who said what. They know who is on the panel, of course. But that is as far as it goes. After that, each expert's argument has to stand on its own merits. Second, an expert is only as good as the arguments she or he gives. So, the central investigator summarizes the arguments and lets the panelists decide if they accept them or not. When consensus appears to be at hand, the central investigator proposes this and asks if people agree. If not, then points of disagreement among the experts are registered. We want to share with you one important example of each of these. First we will describe the expert consensus view of the dispositions which are absolutely vital to good critical thinking. Then we will note a point of separation among the experts.

The Disposition Toward Critical Thinking

What kind of a person would be apt to use their critical thinking skills? The experts poetically describe such a person as having "a critical spirit." Having a critical spirit does not mean that the person is always negative and hypercritical of everyone and everything. The experts use the metaphorical phrase *critical spirit* in a *positive* sense. By it they mean "a probing inquisitiveness, a keenness of mind, a zealous dedication to reason, and a hunger or eagerness for reliable information." Almost sounds like Supreme Court Justice Sandra Day O'Connor or Sherlock Holmes. The kind of person being described here is the kind that always wants to ask "Why?" or "How?" or "What happens if?" The one key difference is that in fiction Sherlock always solves the mystery, while in the real world there is no guarantee. Critical thinking is about how you approach problems, questions, and issues. It is the best way we know of to get to the truth. But! There still are no guarantees – no answers in the back of the book of real life. Does this characterization, that good critical thinkers possess a "critical spirit, a probing inquisitiveness, a keenness of mind...," fit with your examples of people you would call good critical thinkers?

But, you might say, I know people who have skills but do not use them. We cannot call someone a good critical thinker just because she or he has these cognitive skills, however important they might be, because what if they just do not bother to apply them?

One response is to say that it is hard to imagine an accomplished dancer who never dances. After working to develop those skills it seems such a shame to let them grow weak with lack of practice. But dancers get tired. And they surrender to the stiffness of age or the fear of injury. In the case of critical thinking skills, we might argue that not using them once you have them is hard to imagine. It's hard to imagine a person deciding not to think.

Considered as a form of thoughtful judgment or reflective decision-making, in a very real sense critical thinking is **pervasive**. There is hardly a time or a place where it would not seem to be of potential value. As long as people have purposes in mind and wish to judge how to accomplish them, as long as people wonder what is true and what is not, what to believe and what to reject, good critical thinking is going to be necessary.

And yet weird things happen, so it is probably true that some people might let their thinking skills grow dull. It is easier to imagine times when people are just too tired, too lax, or too frightened. But imagine it you can, Young Skywalker, so there has to be more to critical thinking than just the list of cognitive skills. Human beings are more than thinking machines. And this brings us back to those all-important attitudes which the experts called "dispositions."

The experts were persuaded that critical thinking is a pervasive and purposeful human phenomenon. The ideal critical thinker can be characterized not merely by her or his cognitive skills but also by how she or he approaches life and living in general. This is a bold claim. Critical thinking goes way beyond the classroom. In fact, many of the experts fear that some of the things people experience in school are actually harmful to the development and cultivation of good critical thinking. Critical thinking came before schooling was ever invented; it lies at the very roots of civilization. It is a cornerstone in the journey humankind is taking from beastly savagery to global sensitivity. Consider what life would be like without the things on this list and we think you will understand. The approaches to life and living which characterize critical thinking include

- inquisitiveness with regard to a wide range of issues
- concern to become and remain well-informed
- alertness to opportunities to use critical thinking
- trust in the processes of reasoned inquiry
- self-confidence in one's own abilities to reason
- open-mindedness regarding divergent world views
- flexibility in considering alternatives and opinions
- understanding of the opinions of other people
- fair-mindedness in appraising reasoning
- honesty in facing one's own biases, prejudices, stereotypes, or egocentric tendencies
- prudence in suspending, making or altering judgments
- willingness to reconsider and revise views where honest reflection suggests that change is warranted.

What would someone be like who lacked those dispositions? It might be someone who does not care about much of anything, is not interested in the facts, prefers not to think, mistrusts reasoning as a way of finding things out or solving problems, holds his or her own reasoning abilities in low esteem, is close-minded, inflexible, insensitive, cannot understand what others think, is unfair when it comes to judging the quality of arguments, denies his or her own biases, jumps to conclusions or delays too long in making judgments, and never is willing to reconsider an opinion. Not someone prudent people would want to ask to manage their investments!

The experts went beyond approaches to life and living in general to emphasize that good critical thinkers can also be described in terms of how they approach specific issues, questions, or problems. The experts said you would find these sorts of characteristics:

- clarity in stating the question or concern
- orderliness in working with complexity
- diligence in seeking relevant information
- reasonableness in selecting and applying criteria.
- care in focusing attention on the concern at hand
- persistence though difficulties are encountered
- precision to the degree permitted by the subject and the circumstances.

So, how would a poor critical thinker approach specific problems or issues? Obviously, by being any of these things:

- muddle-headed about what he or she is doing
- disorganized and overly simplistic
- spotty about getting the facts
- apt to apply unreasonable criteria
- easily distracted
- ready to give up at the least hint of difficulty
- intent on a solution that is more detailed than is possible
- satisfied with an overly generalized and uselessly vague response.

Remind you of anyone you know?

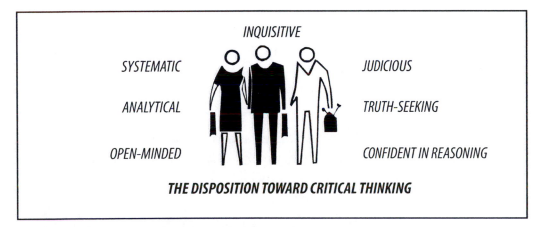

Figure 3 These characteristics represent the qualities of strong critical thinkers.

Someone **strongly** disposed toward critical thinking would probably agree with statements like these:

"I hate talk shows where people shout their opinions but never give any reasons at all."

"Figuring out what people really mean by what they say is important to me."

"I always do better in jobs where I'm expected to think things out for myself."

"I hold off making decisions until I have thought through my options."

"I try to see the merit in another's opinion, even if I reject it later."

"Rather than relying on someone else's notes, I prefer to read the material myself."

"Even if a problem is tougher than I expected, I will keep working on it."

"Making intelligent decisions is more important than winning arguments."

A person with **weak** critical thinking dispositions would probably disagree with the statements above but would be likely to agree with these:

"I prefer jobs where the supervisor says exactly what to do and exactly how to do it."

"No matter how complex the problem, you can bet there will be a simple solution."

"I don't waste time looking things up."

"I hate when teachers discuss problems instead of just giving the answers."

"If my belief is truly sincere, evidence to the contrary is irrelevant."

"Selling an idea is like selling cars: you say whatever works."

We used the expression "strong critical thinker" to contrast with the expression "weak critical thinker." But you will find people who drop the adjective "strong" (or "good") and just say that someone is a "critical thinker" or not. It is like saying that a soccer (European "football") player is a "defender" or "not a defender," instead of saying the player's skills at playing defense are strong or weak. People use the word "defender" in place of the phrase "is good at playing defense." Similarly, people use "critical thinker" in place of "is a good critical thinker" or "has strong critical thinking skills." This is not only a helpful conversational shortcut, it suggests that to many people "critical thinker" has a **laudatory** sense. The word can be used to praise someone at the same time that it identifies the person, as in "Look at that play. That's what I call a defender!"

> *If we were compelled to make a choice between these personal attributes and knowledge about the principles of logical reasoning together with some degree of technical skill in manipulating special logical processes, we should decide for the former.*
>
> *— John Dewey*, How We Think, *1909*

We said the experts did not come to full agreement on something. That thing has to do with the concept of a "good critical thinker." This time the emphasis is on the word "good" because of a crucial ambiguity it contains. A person can be good at critical thinking, meaning that the person can have the appropriate dispositions and be adept at the cognitive processes, while still not being a good (in the moral sense) critical thinker. For example, a person can be adept at developing arguments and then, unethically, use this skill to mislead and exploit a gullible person, perpetrate a fraud, or deliberately confuse and confound, and frustrate a project.

The experts were faced with an interesting problem. Some, a minority, would prefer to think that critical thinking, by its very nature, is inconsistent with the kinds of unethical and deliberately counterproductive examples given. They find it hard to imagine a person who was good at critical thinking not also being good in the broader personal and social sense. In other words, if a person were "really" a "good critical thinker" in the procedural sense and if the person had all the appropriate dispositions, then the person simply would not do those kinds of exploitive and aggravating things.

The large majority, however, hold the opposite judgment. They are firm in the view that good critical thinking has nothing to do with any given set of cultural beliefs, religious tenants, ethical values, social mores, political orientations, or orthodoxies of any kind. Rather, the commitment one makes as a good critical thinker is to always seek the truth with objectivity, integrity, and fair-mindedness. The majority of experts maintain that critical thinking conceived of as we have described it above is regrettably not inconsistent with abusing one's knowledge, skills, or power. There have been people with superior thinking skills and strong habits of mind who, unfortunately, have used their talents for ruthless, horrific, and immoral purposes. Would that it were not so. Would that experience, knowledge, mental horsepower, and ethical virtue were all one and the same. But from the time of Socrates, if not thousands of years before that, humans have known that many of us have one or more of these without having the full set.

Any tool, any approach to situations, can go either way, ethically speaking, depending on the character, integrity, and principles of the persons who possess them. So, in the final analysis the majority of experts maintained that we cannot say a person is not thinking critically simply because we disapprove ethically of what the person is doing. The majority concluded that, "What 'critical thinking' means, why it is of value, and the ethics of its use are best regarded as three distinct concerns."

Perhaps this realization forms part of the basis for why people these days are demanding a broader range of learning outcomes from our schools and colleges. "Knowledge and skills," the staples of the educational philosophy of the mid-twentieth century, are not sufficient. We must look to a broader set of outcomes including habits of mind and dispositions, such as civic engagement, concern for the common good, and social responsibility.

"Thinking" in Popular Culture

We have said so many good things about *critical thinking* that you might have the impression that "critical thinking" and "good thinking" mean the same thing. But that is not what the experts said. They see critical thinking as making up part of what we mean by good thinking, but not as being the only kind of good thinking. For example, they would have included creative thinking as part of good thinking.

Creative or *innovative thinking* is the kind of thinking that leads to new insights, novel approaches, fresh perspectives, whole new ways of understanding and conceiving of things. The products of creative thought include some obvious things like music, poetry, dance, dramatic literature, inventions, and technical innovations. But there are some not so obvious examples as well, such as ways of putting a question that expand the horizons of possible solutions, or ways of conceiving of relationships which challenge presuppositions and lead one to see the world in imaginative and different ways.

The experts working on the concept of critical thinking wisely left open the entire question of what the other forms good thinking might take. Creative thinking is only one example. There is a kind of *purposive, kinetic thinking* that instantly coordinates movement and intention as, for example, when an athlete dribbles a soccer ball down the field during a match. There is a kind of *meditative thinking* which may lead to a sense of inner peace or to profound insights about human existence. In contrast, there is a kind of *hyper-alert, instinctive thinking* needed by soldiers in battle. In the context of popular culture one finds people proposing all kinds of thinking or this-kind of intelligence or that-kind of intelligence. Some times it is hard to sort out the science from the pseudo-science, the kernel of enduring truth from the latest cocktail party banter.

"Thinking" in Cognitive Science

Theories emerging from more scientific studies of human thinking and decision-making in recent years propose that thinking is more integrated and less dualistic than the notions in popular culture suggest. We should be cautious about proposals suggesting oversimplified ways of understanding how humans think. We should avoid harsh, rigid dichotomies such as "reason vs. emotion," "intuitive vs. linear," "creativity vs. criticality," "right brained vs. left brained," "as on Mars vs. as on Venus."

There is often a kernel of wisdom in popular beliefs, and perhaps that gem this time is the realization that some times we decide things very quickly almost as spontaneous, intuitive, reactions to the situation at hand. Many accidents on the freeways of this nation are avoided precisely because drivers are able to see and react to dangerous situations so quickly. Many good decisions which feel intuitive are really the fruit of expertise. Decisions good drivers make in those moments of crisis, just like the decisions which practiced athletes make in the flow of a game or the decisions that a gifted teacher makes as she or he interacts with students, are borne of expertise, training, and practice.

At the same time that we are immersed in the world around us and in our daily lives, constantly making decisions unreflectively, we may also be thinking quite reflectively about something. Perhaps we're worried about a decision which we have to make about an important project at work, or about a personal relationship, or about a legal matter, whatever. We gather information, consider our options, explore possibilities, formulate some thoughts about what we propose to do and why this choice is the right one. In other words, we make a purposeful, reflective judgment about what to believe or what to do – precisely the kind of judgment which is the focus of critical thinking.

Recent integrative models of human decision-making propose that the thinking process of our species is not best described as a conflictive duality as in "intuitive vs. reflective" but rather an integrative functioning of two mutually supportive systems "intuitive and reflective." These two systems of thinking are present in all of us and can act in parallel to process cognitively the matters over which we are deciding.

One system is more intuitive, reactive, quick, and holistic. So as not to confuse things with the notions of thinking in popular culture, cognitive scientists often name this system "System 1." The other (yes, you can guess its name) is more deliberative, reflective, computational and rule governed. You are right; it is called "System 2."

In System 1 thinking, one relies heavily on a number of heuristics (cognitive maneuvers), key situational characteristics, readily associated ideas, and vivid memories to arrive quickly and confidently at a judgment. System 1 thinking is particularly helpful in familiar situations when time is short and immediate action is required.

While System 1 is functioning, another powerful system is also at work, that is, unless we shut it down by abusing alcohol or drugs, or with fear or indifference. **Called "System 2," this is our more reflective thinking system. It is useful for making judgments when you find yourself in unfamiliar situations and have more time to figure things out. It allows us to process abstract concepts, to deliberate, to plan ahead, to consider options carefully, to review and revise our work in the light of relevant guidelines or standards or rules of procedure.** While System 2 decisions are also influenced by the correct or incorrect application of heuristic maneuvers, this is the system which relies on well-articulated reasons and more fully developed evidence.

It is reasoning based on what we have learned through careful analysis, evaluation, explanation, and self-correction. This is the system which values intellectual honesty, analytically anticipating what happens next, maturity of judgment, fair-mindedness, elimination of biases, and truth-seeking. This is the system which we rely on to think carefully through complex, novel, high-stakes, and highly integrative problems.[3] Educators urge us to improve our critical thinking skills and to reinforce our disposition to use those skills because that is perhaps the best way to develop and refine our System 2 reasoning.

System 1 and System 2 are both believed to be vital decision-making tools when stakes are high and when uncertainty is an issue. Each of these two cognitive systems is believed to be capable of functioning to monitor and potentially override the other. This is one of the ways our species reduces the chance of making foolish, sub-optimal or even dangerous errors in judgment. Human thinking is far from perfect. Even a good thinker makes both System 1 and 2 errors. At times we misinterpret things, or we get our facts wrong, and we make mistakes as a result. But often our errors are directly related to the influences and misapplications of *cognitive heuristics*. Because we share the propensity to use these heuristics as we make decisions, let's examine how some of them influence us.

Cognitive heuristics are thinking maneuvers which, at times, appear to be almost hardwired into our species. They influence both systems of thinking, the intuitive thinking of System 1 and the reflective reasoning of System 2. Five heuristics often seen to be more frequently operating in our System 1 reasoning are known as *availability, affect, association, simulation,* and *similarity.*

Availability, the coming to mind of a story or vivid memory of something that happened to you or to someone close to you, inclines a person to make inaccurate estimates of the likelihood of that thing's happening again. People tell stories of things that happened to themselves or their friends all the time as a way of explaining their own decisions. The stories may not be scientifically representative; the events may be mistaken, misunderstood, or misinterpreted. But all that aside, the power of the story is to guide, often in a good way, the decision toward one choice rather than another.

The **Affect** heuristic operates when you have an immediate positive or a negative reaction to some idea, proposal, person, object, whatever. Sometimes called a "gut reaction," this affective response sets up an initial orientation in us, positive or negative, toward the object. It takes a lot of System 2 reasoning to overcome a powerful affective response to an idea, but it can be done. And at times it should be, because there is no guarantee that your gut reaction is always right.

The **Association** heuristic is operating when one word or idea reminds us of something else. For example, some people associate the word "cancer" with "death." Some associate "sunshine" with "happiness." These kinds of associational reasoning responses can be helpful at times, as for example if associating cancer with death leads you not to smoke and to go in for regular checkups. At other times the same association may influence a person to make an unwise decision, as for example if associating "cancer" with "death" were to lead you to be so fearful and pessimistic that you do not seek diagnosis and treatment of a worrisome cancer symptom until it was really too late to do anything.

The **Simulation** heuristic is working when you are imagining how various scenarios will unfold. People often imagine how a conversation will go, or how they will be treated by someone else when they meet the person, or what their friends or boss or lover will say and do when they have to address some difficult issue. These simulations, like movies in our heads, help us prepare and do a better job when the difficult moment arrives. But they can also lead us to have mistaken

Even if you don't remember the name "System 1 thinking," remember the circumstances when you think this way – "when time is short and immediate action is required."

expectations. People may not respond as we imagined; things may go much differently. Our preparations may fail us because the ease of our simulation misled us into thinking that things would have to go as we had imagined them. And they did not.

The **Similarity** heuristic operates when we notice some way in which we are like someone else and infer that what happened to that person is therefore more likely to happen to us. The similarity heuristic functions much like an analogical argument or metaphorical model. The similarity we focus on might be fundamental and relevant, which would make the inference more warranted. For example, the boss fired your coworker for missing sales targets and you draw the reasonable conclusion that if you miss your sales targets you'll be fired, too. Or the similarity that comes to mind might be superficial or not connected with the outcome, which would make the inference unwarranted. For example, you see a TV commercial showing trim-figured young people enjoying fattening fast foods and infer that because you're young too you can indulge your cravings for fast foods without gaining a lot of excess unsightly poundage.

Heuristics and biases often appearing to be somewhat more associated with System 2 thinking include: *satisficing, risk/loss aversion, anchoring with adjustment,* and *the illusion of control.*

Satisficing occurs as we consider our alternatives. When we come to one which is good enough to fulfill our objectives, we often regard ourselves as having completed our deliberations. We have satisficed. And why not? The choice is, after all, good enough. It may not be perfect, it may not be optimal, it may not even be the best among the options available. But it is good enough. Time to decide and move forward.

The running mate of satisficing is temporizing. Temporizing is deciding that the option which we have come to is "good enough for now." We often move through life satisficing and temporizing. At times we look back on our situations and wonder why it is that we have settled for far less than we might have. If we had only studied harder, worked out a little more, taken better care of ourselves and our relationships, perhaps we would not be living as we are now. But, at the time each of the decisions along the way was "good enough for the time being."

We are by nature a species that is **averse to risk and loss**. Often we make decisions on the basis of what we are too worried about losing, rather than on the basis of what we might gain. This works out to be a rather serviceable approach in many circumstances. People do not want to lose control, they do not want to lose their freedom, they do not want to lose their lives, their families, their jobs, their possessions. High stakes gambling is best left to those who can afford to lose the money. Las Vegas didn't build all those multi-million dollar casino hotels because vacationers are winning all the time! And so, in real life, we take precautions. We avoid unnecessary risks. The odds may not be stacked against us, but the consequences of losing at times are so great that we would prefer to forego the possibilities of gain in order not to lose what we have. And yet, on occasion this can be a

System 2 thinking occurs when you have more time and you can reflect and consider options. Try to be a System 2 thinker when it comes to your study routines.

most unfortunate decision, too. History has shown time and time again that businesses which avoid risks often are unable to compete successfully with those willing to move more boldly into new markets or into new product lines.

Any heuristic is only a maneuver, perhaps a shortcut or impulse to think or act in one way rather than another, but certainly not a failsafe rule. It may work out well much of the time to rely on the heuristic, but it will not work out for the best all of the time.

For example, people with something to lose tend toward conservative choices politically as well as economically. Nothing wrong with that necessarily. Just an observation about the influence of Loss Aversion heuristic on actual decision-making. We are more apt to endure the status quo, even as it slowly deteriorates, than we are to call for "radical" change. Regrettably, however, when the call for change comes, it often requires a far greater upheaval to make the necessary transformations, or on occasion, the situation has deteriorated beyond the point of no return. In those situations we find ourselves wondering why we waited so long before doing something.

The heuristic known as **Anchoring with Adjustment** is operative when we find ourselves making evaluative judgments. The natural thing for us to do is to locate or anchor our evaluation at some point along whatever scale we are using. For example, a professor says that the student's paper is a C+. Then, as other information comes our way, we may adjust that judgment. The professor, for example, may decide that the paper is as good as some others that were given a B-, and so adjust the grade upward. The interesting thing about this heuristic, is that we do not normally start over with a fresh evaluation. We have dropped anchor and we may drag it upward or downward a bit, but we do not pull it off the bottom of the sea to relocate our evaluation. First impressions, as the saying goes, cannot be undone. The good thing about this heuristic is that it permits us to move on. We have done the evaluation; there are other papers to grade, other projects to do, other things in life that need attention. We could not long endure if we had to constantly reevaluate every thing anew. The unfortunate thing about this heuristic is that we sometimes drop anchor in the wrong place; we have a hard time giving people a second chance at making a good first impression.

The heuristic known as **Illusion of Control** is evident in many situations. Many of us overestimate our abilities to control what will happen. We make plans for how we are going to do this or that, say this or that, manipulate the situation this way or that way, share or not share this information or that possibility, all the time thinking that some how our petty plans will enable us to control what happens. We act as if others are dancing on the ends of the strings that we are pulling, when in actuality the influences our words or actions have on future events may be quite negligible. At times we do have some measure of control. For example we may exercise, not smoke, and watch our diet in order to be more fit and healthy. We are careful not to drink if we are planning to drive so that we reduce the risks of being involved in a traffic accident. But at times we simply are mistaken about our ability to actually exercise full control over a situation. Sadly we might become ill even if we do work hard to take good care of ourselves. Or we may be involved in an accident even if we are sober. Our business may fail even if we work very hard to make it a success. We may not do as well on an exam as we might hope even if we study hard.

Related to the Illusion of Control heuristic is the tendency to misconstrue our personal influence or responsibility for past events. This is called **Hindsight Bias.** We may overestimate the influence our actions have had on events when things go right, or we may underestimate our responsibility or culpability when things go wrong. We have all heard people bragging about how they did this and how they did that and, as a result, such and such wonderful things happened. We made these great plans and look how well our business did financially. That may be true when the economy is strong, but not when the economy is failing. It is not clear how much of that success came from the planning and how much came from the general business environment. Or, we have all been in the room when it was time to own up for some thing that went wrong and thought to ourselves, hey, I may have had some part in this, but it was not entirely my fault. "It wasn't my fault the children were late for school. Hey, I was dressed and ready to go at the regular time" – as if seeing that the family was running late I had no responsibility to take some initiative and help out.

Research on our shared heuristic patterns of decision-making does not aim to evaluate these patterns as necessarily good or bad patterns of thinking. I fear that my wording of them above may not have been as entirely neutral and descriptive as perhaps it should have been. In truth, reliance on heuristics can be an efficient ways of deciding things, given how very complicated our lives are. We cannot devote maximal cognitive resources to every single decision we make.

Insanity is doing the same thing over and over again while expecting a different outcome.

– Albert Einstein

Those of us who study these heuristic thinking phenomena are simply trying to document how we humans *do* think. There are many useful purposes for doing this. For example, if we find that people repeatedly make a given kind of mistake when thinking about a commonly experienced problem, then we might find ways to intervene and to help ourselves not repeat that error over and over again.

This research on the actual patterns of thinking used by individuals and by groups might prove particularly valuable to those who seek interventions which could improve how we make our own health care decisions, how we make business decisions, how we lead teams of people to work more effectively in collaborative settings, and the like.

Popular culture offers one other myth about decision-making which is worth questioning. And that is the belief that when we make reflective decisions we carefully weigh each of our options, giving due consideration to all of them in turn before deciding which we will adopt.

Although perhaps it should be, research on human decision-making shows that this simply is not what happens.[4]

When seeking to explain how people decide on an option with such conviction that they stick to their decision over time and with such confidence that they act on that decision, the concept that what we do is build a **Dominance Structure** has been put forth. In a nutshell this theory suggests that when we settle on a particular option which is good enough we tend to elevate its merits and diminish its flaws relative to the other options. We raise it up in our minds until it becomes for us the dominant option. In this way, as our decision takes shape, we gain confidence in our choice and we feel justified in dismissing the other options, even though the objective distance between any of them and our dominant option may not be very great at all. But we become invested in our dominant option to the extent that we are able to put the other possibilities aside and act on the basis of our choice. In fact, it comes to dominate the other options in our minds so much that we are able to sustain our decision to act over a period of time, rather than going back to re-evaluate or reconsider constantly. Understanding the natural phenomenon of dominance structuring can help us appreciate why it can be so difficult for us to get others to change their minds, or why it seems that our reasons for our decisions are so much better than any of the objections which others might make to our decisions. This is not to say that we are right or wrong. Rather, this is only to observe that human beings are capable of unconsciously building up defenses around their choices which can result in the warranted or unwarranted confidence to act on the basis of those choices.

Realizing the power of dominance structuring, one can only be more committed to the importance of education and critical thinking. We should do all that we can to inform ourselves fully and to reflect carefully on our choices before we make them, because we are, after all, human and we are as likely as the next person to believe that we are right and they are wrong once the dominance structure begins to be erected. Breaking through that to fix bad decisions, which is possible, can be much harder than getting things right in the first place.

There are more heuristics than only those mentioned above. There is more to learn about dominance structuring as it occurs in groups as well as in individuals, and how to mitigate the problems which may arise by prematurely settling on a "good enough" option, or about how to craft educational programs or interventions which help people be more effective in their System 1 and System 2 thinking. There is much to learn about human thinking and how to optimize it in individuals of different ages; how to optimize the thinking of groups of peers and groups where organizational hierarchies influence interpersonal dynamics. And, happily, there is a lot we know today about human thinking and decision-making that we did not know a few years ago.

This is what we do when we "talk ourselves into an idea." This is sometimes called rationalizing or justifying, and we use it in lots of situations – from "doing what we want" to "speaking our mind." Sometimes it's a good thing; sometimes it isn't. Before you disregard all of your other options in favor of the one that "sounds" or "looks the best," ask yourself if this is the Dominance Structure process at work.

Which brings us to the final question, "Why is critical thinking of particular value?"

Let us start with you first. Why would it be of value to you to have the cognitive skills of interpretation, analysis, evaluation, inference, explanation, and self-regulation?

Why would it be of value to you to learn to approach life and to approach specific concerns with the critical thinking dispositions listed above? Would you have greater success in your work? Would you get better grades?

Actually the answer to the grades question, scientifically speaking, is very possibly, Yes! A study of over 1100 college students shows that scores on a college-level critical thinking skills test significantly correlated with college GPA.[5] It has also been shown that critical thinking skills can be learned, which suggests that as one learns them one's GPA might well improve. In further support of this hypothesis is the significant correlation between critical thinking and reading comprehension. Improvements in the one are paralleled by improvements in the other. Now, if you can read better and think better, might you not do better in your classes, learn more, and get better grades? It is, to say the least, very plausible.

> *Learning, critical thinking, and our nation's future: The future now belongs to societies that organize themselves for learning.... Nations that want high incomes and full employment must develop policies that emphasize the acquisition of knowledge and skills by everyone, not just a select few.*
> —*Ray Marshall and Marc Tucker,* Thinking for a Living: Education and the Wealth of Nations

But what a limited benefit – better grades. Who really cares in the long run? Two years after college, five years out, what does GPA really mean? Right now college-level technical and professional programs have a half-life of about four years, which means that the technical content is expanding so fast and changing so much that in about four years after graduation your professional training will be in serious need of renewal. So, if the only thing a college is good for is to get the entry-level training and the credential needed for some job, then college would be a time-limited value.

Is that the whole story? A job is a good thing, but is that what a college education is all about – getting started in a good job? Maybe some cannot see its further value, but many do. A main purpose, if not *the* main purpose, of the collegiate experience, at either the two-year or the four-year level, is to achieve what people have called a "liberal education." Not liberal in the sense of a smattering of this and that for no particular purpose except to fulfill the unit requirement. But liberal in the sense of "liberating." And who is being liberated? You! Liberated from a kind of slavery. But from whom? From professors. Actually, from dependence on professors so that they no longer stand as infallible authorities delivering opinions beyond our capacity to challenge, question, and dissent. In fact, this is exactly what the professors want.

They want their students to excel on their own, to go beyond what is currently known, to make their own contributions to knowledge and to society. [Being a professor is a curious job — the more effective you are as a teacher, the less your students require your aid in learning.]

Critical thinking is the process of purposeful, self-regulatory judgment. This process reasoned consideration to evidence, context, conceptualizations, methods, and criteria.

– The APA Delphi Report, Critical Thinking: A Statement of Expert Consensus for Purposes of Educational Assessment and Instruction

Liberal education is about learning to learn, to think for yourself, on your own and in collaboration with others. Liberal education leads us away from naïve acceptance of authority, above self-defeating relativism, and beyond ambiguous contextualism. It culminates in principled reflective judgment. Learning critical thinking, cultivating the critical spirit, is not just a means to this end; it is part of the goal itself. People who are poor critical thinkers, who lack the dispositions and skills described, cannot be said to be liberally educated, regardless of the academic degrees they may hold.

Yes, there is much more to a liberal education than critical thinking. There is an understanding of the methods, principles, theories, and ways of achieving knowledge which are proper to the different intellectual realms. There is an encounter with the cultural, artistic, and spiritual dimensions of life. There is the evolution of one's decision making to the level of principled integrity and concern for the common good and social justice. There is the realization of the ways all our lives are shaped by global as well as local political, social, psychological, economic, environmental, and physical forces. There is the growth that comes from the interaction with cultures, languages, ethnic groups, religions, nationalities, and social classes other than one's own. There is the refinement of one's humane sensibilities through reflection on the recurring questions of human existence, meaning, love, life and death. There is the sensitivity, appreciation, and critical appraisal of all that is good and all that is bad in the human condition. As the mind awakens and matures, and the proper nurturing and educational nourishment is provided, these other central parts of a liberal education develop as well. Critical thinking plays an essential role in achieving these purposes.

Anything else? What about going beyond the individual to the community?

The experts say critical thinking is fundamental to, if not essential for, "a rational and democratic society." What might the experts mean by this?

Well, how wise would democracy be if people abandoned critical thinking? Imagine an electorate that cared not for the facts, that did not wish to consider the pros and cons of the issues, or if they did, had not the brain power to do so. Imagine your life and the lives of your friends and family placed in the hands of juries and judges who let their biases and stereotypes govern their decisions, who do not attend to the evidence, who are not interested in reasoned inquiry, who do not know how to draw an inference or evaluate one. Without critical thinking people would be more easily exploited not only politically but economically. The impact of abandoning critical thinking would not be confined to the micro-economics of the household checking account. Suppose the people involved in international commerce were lacking in critical thinking skills; they would be unable to analyze and interpret the market trends, evaluate the implications of interest fluctuations, or explain the potential impact of those factors which influence large-scale production and distribution of goods and materials. Suppose these people were unable to draw the proper inferences from the economic facts, or unable to properly evaluate the claims made by the unscrupulous and misinformed. In such a situation serious economic mistakes would be made. Whole sectors of the economy would become unpredictable, and large-scale economic disaster would become extremely likely. So, given a society that does not value and cultivate critical thinking, we might reasonably expect that in time the judicial system and the economic system would collapse. And, in such a society, one that does not liberate its citizens by teaching them to think critically for themselves, it would be madness to advocate democratic forms of government.

> *We understand critical thinking to be purposeful, self-regulatory judgment which results in interpretation, analysis, evaluation, and inference, as well as explanation of the evidential, conceptual, methodological, criteriological, or contextual considerations upon which that judgment is based. CT is essential as a tool of inquiry. As such, CT is a liberating force in education and a powerful resource in one's personal and civic life. While not synonymous with good thinking, CT is a pervasive and self-rectifying human phenomenon. The ideal critical thinker is habitually inquisitive, well-informed, trustful of reason, open-minded, flexible, fair-minded in evaluation, honest in facing personal biases, prudent in making judgments, willing to reconsider, clear about issues, orderly in complex matters, diligent in seeking relevant information, reasonable in the selection of criteria, focused in inquiry, and persistent in seeking results which are as precise as the subject and the circumstances of inquiry permit. Thus, educating good critical thinkers means working toward this ideal. It combines developing CT skills with nurturing those dispositions which consistently yield useful insights and which are the basis of a rational and democratic society.*
>
> *– The APA Delphi Report,* Critical Thinking: A Statement of Expert Consensus for Purposes of Educational Assessment and Instruction

Is it any wonder that business and civic leaders are maybe even more interested in critical thinking than educators? Critical thinking employed by an informed citizenry is a necessary condition for the success of democratic institutions and for competitive free-market economic enterprise. These values are so important that it is in the national interest that we should try to educate all citizens so that they can learn to think critically. Not just for their own personal good, but for the good of the rest of us, too.

Generalizing, imagine a society, say, for example, the millions of people living in the Los Angeles basin, or in New York and along the east coast, or in Chicago, or Mexico City, Cairo, Rome, Tokyo, Baghdad, Moscow, Beijing, or Hong Kong. They are, de facto, entirely dependent upon one another, and on hundreds of thousands of other people as well for their external supplies of food and water, for their survival. Now imagine that these millions permitted their schools and colleges to stop teaching people how to think critically and effectively. Imagine that because of war, or AIDS, or famine, or religious conviction, parents could not or would not teach their children how to think critically. Imagine the social and political strife, the falling apart of fundamental systems of public safety and public health, the loss of any scientific understanding of disease control or agricultural productivity, the emergence of paramilitary gangs, strong men, and petty warlords seeking to protect themselves and their own by acquiring control over what food and resources they can and destroying those who stand in their path.

Look at what has happened around the world in places devastated by economic embargoes, one-sided warfare, or the AIDS epidemic. Or, consider the problem of global warming and how important it is for all of us to cooperate with efforts to curtail our uses of fossil fuels in order to reduce emissions of greenhouse gases.

Consider the "cultural revolutions" undertaken by totalitarian rulers. Notice how in virtually every case absolutist and dictatorial despots seek ever more severe limitations on free expression. They label "liberal" intellectuals "dangers to society" and expel "radical" professors from teaching posts because they might "corrupt the youth." Some use the power of their governmental or religious authority to crush not only their opposition but the moderates as well – all in the name of maintaining the purity of their movement. They intimidate journalists and those media outlets which dare to comment "negatively" on their political and cultural goals or their heavy-handed methods.

The historical evidence is there for us to see what happens when schools are closed or converted from places of education to places for indoctrination. We know what happens when children are no longer being taught truth-seeking, the skills of good reasoning, or the lessons of human history and basic science: Cultures disintegrate; communities collapse; the machinery of civilization fails; massive numbers of people die; and sooner or later social and political chaos ensues.

Or, imagine a media, a religious or political hegemony which cultivated, instead of critical thinking, all the opposite dispositions? Or consider if that hegemony reinforced uncritical, impulsive decision-making and the "ready-shoot-aim" approach to executive action. Imagine governmental structures, administrators, and community leaders who, instead of encouraging critical thinking, were content to make knowingly irrational, illogical, prejudicial, unreflective, shortsighted, and unreasonable decisions.

How long might it take for the people in this society which does not value critical thinking to be at serious risk of foolishly harming themselves and each other?

In 2007 world news reports spoke of school buildings and teachers being shot by terrorists and violently extreme religious zealots. Education which includes a good measure of critical thinking skills and dispositions like truth-seeking and open-mindedness is a problem for terrorists and extremists because they want to have complete control of what people think. Their methods include indoctrination, intimidation, and the strictest authoritarian orthodoxy. In the "black-and-white" world of "us vs. them," a good education would mean that the people might begin to think for themselves. And that is something these extremists do not want.

History shows that assaults on learning, whether by book burning, exile of intellectuals, or regulations aimed at suppressing research and frustrating the fair-minded, evidence-based, and unfettered pursuit of knowledge, can happen wherever and whenever people are not vigilant defenders of open, objective, and independent inquiry.

Does this mean that society should place a very high value on critical thinking? Absolutely.

Does this mean society has the right to force someone to learn to think critically? Maybe.

But, really, should we have to?

ABOUT THE AUTHOR

Dr. Peter A. Facione and his co-investigators have been engaged in research and teaching about reasoning, decision-making, and effective individual and group thinking processes since 1967. Over the years they developed instruments to measure the core skills and habits of mind of effective thinking; these instruments are now in use in many different languages throughout the world. They are available through http://www.insightassessment.com, as are other reports and teaching materials. Since 1992 Dr. Facione has presented hundreds of workshops about effective teaching for thinking and about leadership, decision-making, leadership development, planning and budgeting, and learning outcomes assessment at national and international professional association meetings and on college and university campuses throughout the nation. Dr. Facione is former Provost at Loyola University Chicago and a Senior Scholar with the National Center for Science and Civic Engagement. A philosopher, he earned his Ph.D. at Michigan State, chaired the Department of Philosophy at Bowling Green State University, and served as Dean of the School of Human Development and Community Service at California State University Fullerton before joining Santa Clara University in 1990. At Santa Clara, he was Dean of the College of Arts and Sciences and Director of the Graduate Division of Counseling Psychology and Education for many years. Dr. Facione served as the President of the American Conference of Academic Deans. He has been on many boards and panels, including the California Commission on Teacher Credentialing and the ACE Presidents Task Force on Education. In 2005 he became Senior Director for Academic Leadership with Keeling and Associates, a higher education consulting firm. He teaches at Loyola University Chicago.

ENDNOTES

[1] The quotation from John Chaffee is from *Conversations with Critical Thinkers,* John Esterle and Dan Clurman (Eds.). Whitman Institute. San Francisco, CA. 1993.

[2] The findings of expert consensus cited or reported in this essay are published in *Critical Thinking: A Statement of Expert Consensus for Purposes of Educational Assessment and Instruction.* Peter A. Facione, principle investigator, The California Academic Press, Millbrae, CA, 1990. (ERIC ED 315 423). In 1993/94 the Center for the Study of Higher Education at The Pennsylvania State University undertook a study of 200 policy-makers, employers, and faculty members from two-year and four-year colleges to determine what this group took to be the core critical thinking skills and habits of mind. The Pennsylvania State University Study, under the direction of Dr. Elizabeth Jones, was funded by the U.S. Department of Education Office of Educational Research and Instruction. The Penn State study findings, published in 1994, confirmed the expert consensus described in this paper.

[3] To learn more about this integrative model of thinking and about cognitive heuristics, you may wish to consult the references listed at the end of this essay. The material presented in this section is derived from these books and related publications by many of these same authors and others working to scientifically explain how humans actually make decisions.

[4] Henry Montgomery, "From cognition to action: The search for dominance in decision making." In *Process and Structure in Human Decision-Making*, Montgomery H., Svenson O. (Eds). John Wiley & Sons: Chichester, UK, 1989.

[5] Findings regarding the effectiveness of critical thinking instruction, and correlations with GPA and reading ability are reported in "Technical Report #1, Experimental Validation and Content Validity" (ERIC ED 327 549), "Technical Report #2, Factors Predictive of CT Skills" (ERIC ED 327 550), and "Gender, Ethnicity, Major, CT Self-Esteem, and the California Critical Thinking Skills Test" (ERIC ED 326 584). All by Peter A. Facione and published by the California Academic Press, Millbrae, CA, 1990. These reports are available as PDF files downloadable from www.insightassessment.com/articles3.html or from the author via e-mail attachments.

READINGS

American Philosophical Association, *Critical Thinking: A Statement of Expert Consensus for Purposes of Educational Assessment and Instruction.* "The Delphi Report," Committee on Pre-College Philosophy. (ERIC Doc. No. ED 315 423). 1990

Brookfield, Stephen D. *Developing Critical Thinkers: Challenging Adults to Explore Alternative Ways of Thinking and Acting.* Josey-Bass Publishers: San-Francisco, CA, 1987.

Browne, M. Neil, and Keeley, Stuart M.: *Asking the Right Questions.* Prentice-Hall Publishers: Englewood Cliffs, NJ, 2003.

Costa, Arthur L., & Lowery, Lawrence F.: *Techniques for Teaching Thinking.* Critical Thinking Press and Software: Pacific Grove, CA, 1989.

Dewey, John. *How We Think: A Restatement of the Relation of Reflective Thinking to the Educational Process.* D. C. Heath Publishing: Lexington, MA, 1933.

Facione, Noreen C. and Facione, P.A.: *Critical Thinking Assessment and Nursing Education*

Programs: An Aggregate Data Analysis. The California Academic Press: Millbrae, CA, 1997.

Facione, N.C., and Facione, P.A., Analyzing Explanations for Seemingly Irrational Choices, *International Journal of Applied Philosophy*, Vol. 15 No. 2 (2001) 267-86.

Facione, P.A., Facione N.C., and Giancarlo, C.: The Disposition Toward Critical Thinking: Its Character, Measurement, and Relationship to Critical Thinking Skills, *Journal of Informal Logic,* Vol. 20 No. 1 (2000) 61-84.

Gilovich, Thomas, Griffin, Dale, and Kahneman, Daniel: *Heuristics and Biases: The Psychology of Intuitive Judgment*. Cambridge University Press. 2002.

Goldstein, William, and Hogarth, Robin M. (Eds.): *Research on Judgment and Decision Making*. Cambridge University Press. 1997.

Esterle, John, and Clurman, Dan: *Conversations with Critical Thinkers*. The Whitman Institute: San Francisco, CA, 1993.

Janis, I.L. and Mann, L: *Decision-Making*. The Free Press, New York. 1977.

Kahneman, Daniel; Slovic, Paul; and Tversky, Amos: *Judgment Under Uncertainty: Heuristics and Biases*. Cambridge University Press. 1982.

Kahneman Daniel: Knetsch, J.L.; and Thaler, R.H.: The endowment effect, loss aversion, and status quo bias. *Journal of Economic Perspectives*. 1991, 5;193-206.

King, Patricia M. & Kitchener, Karen Strohm: *Developing Reflective Judgment.* Josey-Bass Publishers: San Francisco, CA, 1994.

Kurfiss, Joanne G., *Critical Thinking: Theory, Research, Practice and Possibilities,* ASHE-ERIC Higher Education Report # 2, Washington DC, 1988.

Marshall, Ray, and Tucker, Marc, *Thinking for a Living: Education and the Wealth of Nations*, Basic Books: New York, NY, 1992.

Resnick, L. W., *Education and Learning to Think,* National Academy Press, 1987.

Rice, Ann. *The Vampire Lestat.* Ballantine Books: New York, NY, 1985.

Rubenfeld, M. Gaie, & Scheffer, Barbara K., *Critical Thinking in Nursing: An Interactive Approach*. J. B. Lippincott Company: Philadelphia, PA, 1995.

Siegel, Harvey: Educating Reason: Rationality, CT and Education. Routledge Publishing: New York, 1989.

Sternberg, Robert J.: *Critical Thinking: Its Nature, Measurement, and Improvement.* National Institute of Education: Washington DC, 1986.

Toulmin, Stephen: *The Uses of Argument*. Cambridge University Press, 1969.

Wade, Carole, and Tavris, Carol: *Critical & Creative Thinking: The Case of Love and War*. Harper Collins College Publisher: New York, NY, 1993.

GOVERNMENT REPORTS

U.S. Department of Education, Office of Educational Research and Improvement, National Center for Educational Statistics (NCES) Documents National Assessment of College Student Learning: Getting Started, A Summary of Beginning Activities. NCES 93-116.

National Assessment of College Student Learning: Identification of the Skills to Be Taught, Learned, and Assessed, A Report on the Proceedings of the Second Design Workshop, November 1992. NCES 94-286.

National Assessment of College Student Learning: Identifying College Graduates' Essential Skills in Writing, Speech and Listening, and Critical Thinking. NCES 95-001.

Questions for Consideration about Critical Thinking

1) What is critical thinking? Define the concept and provide an example not presented in the text where critical thinking would be needed.

_____

_____

_____

_____

2) What are the six core skills associated with critical thinking? Identify each skill and provide a brief explanation of how it functions in a situation requiring critical thinking.

_____

_____

_____

_____

_____

_____

3) What are the characteristics of a strong critical thinker?

_____

_____

_____

4) What are the characteristics of a weak critical thinker?

_____

_____

_____

5) Are you a strong critical thinker or a weak critical thinker? Explain how you came to this conclusion.

_____

_____

_____

_____

6) What is creative thinking? When a person thinks creatively, what can it lead to?

_____

_____

_____

_____

7) What happens when one uses purposive, kinetic thinking?

_____

_____

_____

_____

8) What is the result of meditative thinking?

_____

_____

_____

_____

9) What is the purpose of instinctive thinking?

_____

_____

_____

_____

10) What happens in System 1 thinking? When are you most likely to use System 1 thinking?

_____

_____

_____

_____

_____

11) What happens in System 2 thinking? When are you most likely to use System 2 thinking?

_____

_____

_____

_____

_____

12) What is a cognitive heuristic?

_____

_____

13) What are the five heuristics most often associated with System 1 thinking? List and describe each one.

_____

_____

_____

_____

_____

_____

_____

_____

_____

14) What are the four heuristics most often associated with System 2 thinking? List and describe each one.

_____

_____

_____

_____

_____

_____

_____

15) Why is critical thinking valuable?

_____

_____

_____
_____
_____
_____
_____

16) Reflect on the ways in which strong critical thinking skills can benefit while you are in school. On your job. With your friends. In your life.

_____
_____
_____
_____
_____
_____
_____
_____
_____
_____
_____
_____
_____
_____
_____
_____

The Art of Critical Reading   **6**

Your world is filled with messages. When you read a book, you see words and images (photos, diagrams, charts, tables, and/or symbols) that convey a message. When you look at an advertisement, you look at images and words that convey a message about a specific product or service. When you surf the Internet, you look at words and images that form electronic messages. When you listen to a speech, you hear words that make up a persuasive message. When you listen to music, you hear words and rhythms that represent the singer's and musician's collaborative efforts to create a melodic message. When you play a video game, you see images and words that create messages about problems that must be solved in order to win the game.

These words and images are called "text." The message contained in a text can be obvious or not so obvious, or both. The obvious message is conspicuous and literal; it relates directly to the words and objects presented in the images. If the text is a magazine article that describes the process of taking care of a cat and includes a photo of a cat, the obvious or literal message is about taking care of a cat. Obvious or literal messages are shaped by obvious elements within the text.

The not-so-obvious message in a text is called a subtext; the subtext is the underlying idea or theme within a text. The subtext can be shaped through the use of color, shapes, size, iconic images or symbols, font style, gender reference, word choice, sentence length, tone, sentence structure, or a host of other devices and techniques with the potential to manipulate the viewer's reaction, and in some cases, motivate the viewer to take action.

Every text has a subtext. Let's look at these examples. Here are two passages of text about the same subject: stress management. Pay close attention to the tone and style of the writing in each passage.

> *EXAMPLE 1:* Stress is defined by psychologists as a series of physiological and psychological responses, predominantly within the nervous, endocrine, and cardiovascular systems of the human body, to stimuli that are perceived as threatening or disturbing. When a body reacts to stress, it triggers a complex series of reactions that cause the body to respond by applying increased tension in the muscles; constricting blood vessels; increasing one's blood sugar levels; dilating the pupils; and dumping significant amounts of the stress hormones adrenaline, norepinephrine, and cortisol into the bloodstream. These bodily reactions prepare the body and mind to protect and defend against danger; this series of behaviors and impulses has been labeled in everyday language the "fight-or-flight" response. While this response mechanism is presumed to protect human beings from danger,

it can have quite the opposite effect if an individual does not know how to manage stress effectively. Prolonged exposure to increased stress hormones and the resultant physical effects can reduce the body's ability to protect itself from physical illness and can encourage the development of psychological conditions such as depression, anxiety, and memory deficits.

The theme of Example 1 is obviously stress, but look more closely. Example 1 has 189 words. The average sentence length is 37.8 words. Four-fifths (80%) of the sentences are constructed in the passive voice. Using the Flesch Reading Ease scale as a guide to determine the relative difficulty of reading, the paragraph ranks at 19.0 – difficult reading. The Reading Ease scale uses values from 0 to 100 to indicate the influence of sentence length and word choice on comprehension; the lower the number, the more difficult the text is to read and understand. Using a similar measurement system, the Flesch-Kincaid Grade Level scale, to evaluate the grade level most likely to comprehend the text, we find the paragraph is ranked at 12.0, or high school senior level.

Example 2 (below) has 207 words. Average sentence length is 21.1 words. All of the sentences are written in active voice. The Flesch Reading Ease score for Example 2 is 79.5 – fairly easy reading. The comprehension level scores at 7.3, or seventh-grade level. Its theme is also stress, but pay attention to the difference in style and tone.

EXAMPLE 2: It's 9 PM the night before the big history exam at 10 AM and you haven't read the chapters in the textbook. You haven't eaten since breakfast and you are ready to chew off your arm when your friends call and invite you out for pizza. But there's that eighty pages that your roommate said was as boring as all get-out and you haven't been to class regularly and you have to read some of the book or else you might just as well not bother to show up and take the F on the exam. As you sit at your desk, trying to decide what to do, you feel your stomach tensing up, your heart beating a whole lot faster, and your head feels like someone has put a rubber band around it and is tightening it more by the minute. You look at the clock. Maybe you can go out and be back by midnight and read all eighty pages and still get a few hours of sleep? Your breathing is getting faster. You are angry that you put off the reading until now. Your stress level is almost off the chart. You wish you were half as responsible as your parents want you to be.

How are the passages alike? How are the passages different? What devices has the writer used within the first example to convey information? What devices has the writer used in the second example to convey information? Are the passages written to appeal to different audiences? Can you speculate what sort of audience would be more interested in the first passage? What sort of audience would be more interested in the second passage? Which article are you more inclined to understand? Why?

Now, let's look at two visual texts and examine them for the messages and themes they contain. The next two pages feature advertisements that focus on the same service: tattoos. Both ads are the same shape and size, and they use the same colors. They use the same image to convey messages about getting a tattoo. Look at them carefully and then respond to the questions related to each ad. Use the list of questions on 67 to guide your analysis.

Passive voice includes forms of the verb "to be" (be, am, is, are, were, being, been).

Active voice includes forms of action verbs.

Compare these two examples:

Passive voice: The attention of the audience was grabbed by the speaker.

Active voice: The speaker grabbed the audience's attention.

Passive voice sounds tired and stilted. Active voice sounds lively and enthusiastic.

Passive voice and "to be" verbs add little to an essay. Active voice and active verbs give an essay energy and vitality.

Take a look at Ad 1. What is the most dominant element in the ad: the photo, the block of handwritten text, the person's name and business title, or the tattoo business's name and phone number? What makes it most dominant?

_____

_____

_____

_____

_____

Now read the text of Ad 1. Do any words in the text stand out when you read them? Why? Are there words or symbols in the text that remind you of other things?

_____

_____

_____

_____

Now look at the photo in Ad 1. What is the most important element in the photo? How have you determined this? What is the least important element in the photo? How have you determined this? What is your reaction to the expression on the woman's face? Why do you think you react this way?

_____

_____

_____

_____

Does the ad motivate you to take action? What does it motivate you to do?

_____

_____

_____

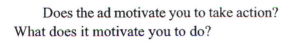

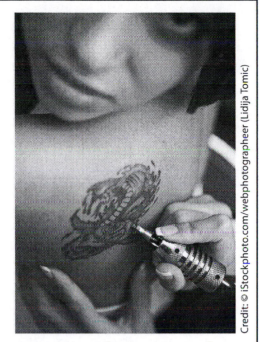

Credit: © iStockphoto.com/webphotographeer (Lidija Tomic)

My tattoo, a dragon wrapped around a rose, says so much about me – strong and tough on the outside, sweet and loving on the inside.

That's what I like about tattoos. They reveal things about us that sometimes words just can't capture. To be able to express my true nature on my skin makes my body a living canvas and my life a thing of beauty.

Tattooing is the perfect way to express myself in color.

Amanda
Office Clerk, Fairleigh School of Business

Figure 4 Ad 1.

Don't. Get. Stuck.

You don't want somebody else's infection. Before you get inked, check the set-up at the tattoo studio.

✔ **Clean workstation?**

✔ **Artist wears sterile gloves?**

✔ **Sterile equipment? Look for brown arrows on the sterilizing pouches.**

✔ **Plastic-covered clip cord?**

✔ **Plastic barriers around items to avoid contamination?**

✔ **Packaged, new needles?**

✔ **New disposable razors?**

Protect. Your. Health.

A public safety announcement from the
**TATTOO SAFETY ASSOCIATION OF
SOUTHERN SASKATCHEWAN**
WWW.TATS2USASK.ORG

Credit: © iStockphoto.com/webphotographeer (Lidija Tomic)

Figure 5 Ad 2.

Look at Ad 2. What is the most dominant element in the ad: the photo, the three-word headline, the checklist, the three-word headline at the bottom of the ad, the small type at the bottom of the ad? What makes it most dominant?

_____

_____

_____

_____

_____

Now read the text of Ad 2. Do any words in the text stand out when you read them? Why? Are there words or symbols in the text that remind you of other things?

_____

_____

_____

_____

Now look at the photo in Ad 2. What is the most important element in the photo? How have you determined this? What is the least important element in the photo? How have you determined this? What is your reaction to the expression on the woman's face? Why do you think you react this way?

_____

_____

_____

_____

Does the ad motivate you to take action? What does it motivate you to do?

_____

_____

_____

_____

Remember: Every text has a subtext. Whether you are reading a magazine, watching a news show, or playing a video game, you need to be aware that the text (words and images) you are seeing is hard at work conveying obvious and not-so-obvious messages to you at the same time. The obvious "text" of literature, art, theater, and film also has a subtext that serves as the underlying theme or message of the work.

But how do you evaluate a text for its obvious and not-so-obvious messages? The University of British Columbia Writing Centre has developed an outstanding list of hints and tips to help you identify techniques and devices writers use to create obvious and not-so-obvious messages. Use this list to help you evaluate the text and subtext in the materials you read for school, on the job, and for fun. As you learn more about critical thinking, rhetoric, and college writing, you will understand the significance of these techniques and devices. As you read a text, ask yourself the questions listed here. By reading a text for its style and form as well as its content, you'll be able to better understand its purpose.

15 Questions to Ask for a Critical Reading

University of British Columbia Writing Centre

1. What is the general subject? Does the subject mean anything to you? Does it bring up any personal associations? Is the subject a controversial one?

2. What is the thesis (the overall main point) of the text? How does the thesis interpret/comment on the subject?

3. What is the tone of the text? Do you react at an emotional level to the text? Does this reaction change at all throughout the text?

4. What is the writer's purpose? To explain? To inform? To anger? Persuade? Amuse? Motivate? Sadden? Ridicule? Anger? Is there more than one purpose? Does the purpose shift at all throughout the text?

5. How does the writer develop his/her ideas? Narration? Description? Definition? Comparison? Analogy? Cause and Effect? Example? Why does the writer use these methods of development?

6. How does the writer arrange his/her ideas? What are the patterns of arrangement? Particular to general? Broad to specific? Spatial? Chronological? Alternating? Block?

7. Is the text unified and coherent? Are there adequate transitions? How do the transitions work?

8. What is the sentence structure like in the text? Does the writer use fragments or run-ons? Declarative? Imperative? Interrogative? Exclamatory? Are they simple? Compound? Complex? Compound-complex? Short? Long? Loose? Periodic? Balanced? Parallel? Are there any patterns in the sentence struc-

ture? Can you make any connections between the patterns and the writer's purpose?

9. Does the writer use dialogue? Quotations? To what effect?

10. How does the writer use diction? Is it formal? Informal? Technical? Jargon? Slang? Is the language connotative? Denotative? Is the language emotionally evocative? Does the language change throughout the piece? How does the language contribute to the writer's aim?

11. Is there anything unusual in the writer's use of punctuation? What punctuation or other techniques of emphasis (italics, capitals, underlining, ellipses, parentheses) does the writer use? Is punctuation over- or under-used? Which marks does the writer use when, and for what effects? Dashes to create a hasty pause? Semicolons for balance or contrast?

12. Are important terms repeated throughout the text? Why?

13. Are there any particularly vivid images that stand out? What effect do these images have on the writer's purpose?

14. Are devices of comparison used to convey or enhance meaning? Which tropes – similes, metaphors, personification, hyperbole, etc. – does the writer use? When does he/she use them? Why?

15. Does the writer use devices of humor? Puns? Irony? Sarcasm? Understatement? Parody? Is the effect comic relief? Pleasure? Hysteria? Ridicule?

A Word About Grammar　7

Remember the word *grammar*? It might have been a word in the title of one of your grade school textbooks. Or it might have been something one (and maybe more!) of your teachers harped on for a few weeks in the fall. For most students, grammar was a snake's nest of rules about when and how and why and where you did what you did when you wrote. Do you remember any of these rules?

- Sentence equals subject plus verb.
- Adverbs are supposed to end in *–ly*.
- *And* is a conjunction that joins two complete thoughts to form a compound sentence.
- Never end a sentence with a preposition.

Is it coming back to you? Good. Grammar represents the structure of a language. It is taught to help students identify the basic forms and styles of a standardized version of a language. *Standardized* means conforming to a standard – in your case, your school's or community's dominant language. Grammar is made up of rules or conventions that form the framework of the standardized version of a language – not the dialects, slang terms, street talk, and other local nuances that form the exceptions, but the standardized version.

Grammar has always been about rules. These rules may have changed over decades and centuries as civilizations, cultures, and the attitudes of academicians have changed, but the rules do not change overnight and you have not been personally appointed to change them. That means that, as a college student, you are expected to appreciate and utilize the standard grammar rules of your school's dominant language.

Because this book is being written in English for English-language schools, the basic grammar rules presented here will adhere to a standardized version of English. If, after reading these rules, your curiosity piques and you want to know more about grammar and all its glorious rules, there are many excellent grammar books on the market that will feed your need to read. A good grammar book can also serve as a good reference tool for you – while you're in college and later on, when you have graduated and are running your own company.

College papers offer lots of potential for grammar problems. If you don't take the time to plan, write, revise, and proofread, there's a good chance that something will go awry in your writing. That something could be your grammar. The tips on the next two pages offer solutions to the most common problems I observed in the classroom. As you write, be aware that many of the mistakes you make can be fixed by slowing down and reading the problem sentence aloud to detect the error. Try restating the sentence a couple of different ways to see which way makes more sense. Refer to a grammar guide if you still aren't sure how to fix a clunky sentence or phrase. Consulting a reference book so that you can present information clearly is worth a lot in the college classroom.

Grammar tips

A complete sentence is composed of a subject and a verb. If a sentence is missing a subject or verb, it is incomplete.

COMPLETE SENTENCE: The <u>shark</u> <u>uses</u> its dorsal fin to stabilize its position while swimming.

INCOMPLETE SENTENCE: The shark's dorsal <u>fin</u> its position while it is swimming.

A simple sentence has a subject and a verb and conveys a single complete thought.

EXAMPLE: Seven <u>men</u> <u>climbed</u> to the top of the mountain in sixteen days.

A compound sentence is created when two simple sentences are joined with a conjunction such as *and, or,* or *but.*

EXAMPLE: <u>Mozart</u> <u>began</u> composing music when he was six, and <u>Beethoven</u> <u>wrote</u> his first composition in his teens.

A compound subject consisting of two subjects joined with the word *and* takes a plural form of the verb.

EXAMPLE: In the novel, <u>George</u> and <u>Lennie</u> travel together from town to town.

When joining two simple sentences with a conjunction, determine if usage of the word *but* will create contradiction of the two ideas. If contradiction is desired, use the word *but.* If your intent is to join two sentences to reinforce an idea, use the word *and* or don't join the sentences.

TWO SIMPLE SENTENCES: In the movie *King Kong*, the giant ape climbed the Empire State Building. Small airplanes buzzed around King Kong like gnats while he clung to the tower.

CONTRADICTORY: In the movie *King Kong*, the giant ape climbed the Empire State Building, **but** small airplanes buzzed around him like gnats while he clung to the tower. *(There's an air of confusion in this sentence because the references to the tower in each phrase suggest that the ape's experiences are related. **But** causes contradiction, suggesting the idea in the second half of the sentences cancels the idea in the first.)*

EXAMPLE OF CLARITY: In the movie *King Kong*, the giant ape climbed the Empire State Building, **and** small airplanes buzzed around him like gnats while he clung to the tower.

Pay attention to subject-verb agreement when a prepositional or other phrase separates the subject and verb.

EXAMPLE: The entire <u>crate</u> of carry-on meals for this flight <u>weighs</u> less than a single passenger.   subject   verb

When using a phrase to modify a subject, avoid ambiguity.

AMBIGUOUS: Writing to earn money to pay the bills, the apartment in the attic of the ramshackle house looked like the only place Lester could afford. *(Writing describes the apartment. The way the sentence is constructed, it appears that the apartment is doing the writing.)*

CORRECT: Writing to earn money to pay the bills, Lester moved into an apartment in the attic of the ramshackle house. *(The word* writing *in the introductory phrase now describes* Lester. *The sentence makes more sense.)*

When using a phrase to modify the main subject of a sentence, be sure that the form of the subject in the phrase agrees in number (and/or gender, when appropriate) with the subject of the sentence.

INCORRECT: When <u>someone</u> makes a living as a teacher, <u>they</u> have to accept long hours and low pay. *(Someone is singular; they is plural.)*

CORRECT: When <u>someone</u> makes a living as a teacher, <u>he</u> or <u>she</u> has to accept long hours and low pay. *(Someone is singular; he or she is singular.)*

CORRECT: A teacher has to accept long hours and low pay. *(Changing or eliminating the modifying phrase eliminates the ambiguity.)*

Avoid stringing together phrases, clauses, and simple and compound sentences so that they form run-on sentences. Read long sentences aloud, identifying natural "pauses" where one sentence can end and another one can start. If you have to take a breath during the reading of a sentence, the sentence is too long. Pay attention to your inclination to pause during natural breaks in the text. End the sentence at a break, and start a new one. Restructure sentences when necessary.

RUN-ON SENTENCE: When the scientists analyzed the data, they determined that the behavior of the chimpanzees whose hands were bound resembled the antics of the little children they had tested previously and made a decision to test further different age groups of people against different age groups of chimps as a way of identifying whether left-handedness in chimps was the result of manual restriction or whether left-handedness was attributable to age, a feature that had been previously identified by a group of Swedish scientists testing for agility of the opposable thumb in juvenile and mature chimps.

CORRECT: Scientists analyzing the data determined that chimpanzees whose hands were bound acted like young children. The scientists decided to test different age groups of people and chimps to determine whether manual restriction or age factored into the behavior. They were aware of only one other related study. A group of Swedish scientists had tested the chimps' agility in the use of their thumbs.

The Importance of Vocabulary

In college you will read lots of articles and books with complex structures, words, and styles. The first few times you read this stuff, you may find your brain glazing over and your whole psyche sinking into a state of despair. You will say out loud to no one in particular, "Are you kidding? Who talks like this?" You will wonder whether you have enough dental floss in the medicine cabinet. You will have curious affectionate thoughts about the cat you left behind with your parents when you moved to college because you were "so over the litter box thing." You will go online and check the news feed on your Facebook account because it suddenly seems terribly important to do so.

Reading articles and books with a complicated writing style can take all the fun out of studying. Whether you're reading the textbook for your English comp class or the article you downloaded from the library database for biology about the left-handedness tendencies in chimpanzees, you are bound to run across words that seem way over your head and writing styles that cannot sustain your interest. What to do, what to do?

First, read manageable sections of text in manageable periods of time. The brain can only absorb so much new information at one time. The more complex the material is, the more challenging it will be for your brain to interpret and analyze new terms, ideas, and data. Taking notes as you read is a way to process the information in another way so that you can "make it yours." Determine what your reading capacity is by reading until you feel your mind getting tired. Take a 15-minute break. While you are taking a break, mentally review what you have read. If something doesn't make sense, jot down notes and questions about the information that doesn't make sense. When you return to the text, look for the information that wasn't clear. If you have to read the text over again, do so. Answer the questions you jotted down in your notes so that your understanding of the text is solid enough to move on to the next section. You may have to read some sections several times in order to understand their meaning.

Next, buy a dictionary and look up words that are unfamiliar. You may think you can figure out the meaning of a word through context – by its placement in a sentence and its immediate proximity to and association with other words around it – but context encourages conjecture or speculation. You won't actually know what a word means until you see its definition in a dictionary. Write out the word and its definition; the physical act of writing requires you to think about the word and its definition so that you can interpret it and reconstruct it on paper. Once you have reconstructed the word and its definition on paper, look at them for several seconds as you say the word and its definition aloud. The act of seeing word and definition as you say them is part of that whole multiple intelligences thing we talked about a few chapters ago; you're processing the information in at least a couple of different ways (definitely visually and verbally, and possibly musically through patterns or rhythms) in order to make it meaningful to you. (You used bodily/kinetic intelligence when you wrote the word and definition on paper.) Finally, use the new word in a sentence or two so that its meaning makes sense in a new context.

After all, part of the point of a college education is to expand your intellectual knowledge base. That means learning new words as well as new information and ideas. When your vocabulary increases, you are more able to carry on conversations with your instructors and professors about the topics they have presented in class. You can ask more concise questions, and give more concise answers, and you are more likely to understand the questions and answers of those around you.

Understand that the new word you have found may not have universal applications. Use it when you write your responses to the reading assignment or in a paper for the class in which you learned it. In your other classes, look and listen for situations in which you might be able to use the new word in the place of a more familiar word. When such an opportunity occurs, use the new word as though it has been with you since birth and listen closely to the way others respond to your usage of it. If your audience doesn't recognize the word or your usage of it, be prepared to explain its meaning. Teaching or explaining something you know to someone else is one of the best ways to be sure that you understand it.

Finally, once you have established that your new word has relevance outside the immediate environment in which you found it, you can start applying it in appropriate situations. Let's say, for example, that you have "discovered" the word *conjecture*, which means a conclusion or opinion based on inconclusive or incomplete information. You discovered it in your history book, but you learned during a biology lecture on the left-handedness of chimpanzees that conjecture in biology refers to a theory or hypothesis that is proposed but has not been tested scientifically. So, *conjecture* has a place in biology class as well. You can start using the word there, as well, at the same time you look for other situations in which to use your new word in your expanded vocabulary.

Here is a list of words that you may want to add to your vocabulary that will help you move closer to greatness while you are in college. Use your dictionary to look up the definition of each word, and then write down the word and its definition in order to "experience" it. Then look at it and say it aloud, and use it in a sentence so that it feels familiar. Set a goal of learning five new words each week, and you will expand your vocabulary by more than two hundred words each year. That in itself will be a great accomplishment.

If you develop a curiosity for more words, you can read study guides for the SAT, ACT, GRE, LSAT and GMAT standardized tests. They often have lengthy word lists that are considered appropriate vocabulary for college-level students. Good luck.

Handy-Dandy Vocabulary List: Words to Know

aberrant	academia	add
abject	accoutrement	adjudicate
abridge	ad	adjunct

adjutant	de facto	foreword
adroit	deceptive	fortuitous
advocacy	decipher	forward
aesthetic	decorum	fruition
affect	deductive	gamble
agency	defamatory	gambol
allegory	denouement	generalization
allude	deterrent	genital
ambiguous	diabolic	genteel
analogy	dialectic	Gentile
analytical	dialogue	grandiloquent
androgyny	diametric	grisly
annotate	Dickensian	grizzly
antithesis	didactic	harangue
approbation	discourse	harbinger
articulate	discredit	havoc
auspicious	discreet	hegemony
banal	discrimination	heuristic
bathos	dogmatic	histogram
belie	dubious	human
bias	effect	humane
bibliography	effusive	hypothesis
bilateral	egregious	idealism
bilingual	egress	illegible
brevity	elicit	illusive
bursar	elude	implicate
cadence	emotional	implicit
calculate	empirical	imply
capitalism	enigma	inclusive
capricious	enthymeme	incomparable
cathartic	epigram	incompatible
cinematography	epilogue	inconspicuous
circumspect	epistolary	inculcate
coalescence	epistemology	inculpate
cogent	epitome	incur
cognitive	equivocate	inductive
colloquial	erudite	infallible
comedy	esoteric	infamous
concept	ethos	infer
conciliatory	etiology	inherent
conclude	evaluate	institutional
conflate	exclusive	interpret
conjecture	explicit	it's
conspicuous	facetious	its
contextualize	fallacy	jargon
convolute	farce	judicious
credibility	feasible	juggler
crux	forgo	jugular
database	foreshadow	juxtapose

kinesics
kinesiology
kinetic
labyrinth
lackluster
laconism
latent
lax
legible
levity
lexicon
logic
logo
logos
loquacious
maniacal
mantel
mantle
marginalize
maudlin
metaphor
metaphysical
misanthrope
misconception
misinterpret
misnomer
misogamy
misogyny
misology
misperception
missive
mnemonic
moot
mythos
narrative
nascent
negate
nominalism
nuance
objective
oblique
obstreperous
obtrusive
Occam's razor
occlude
ontology
ordinance

ordnance
oscillate
pander
paraphrase
pathos
paucity
peak
peek
pejorative
perspicacity
pervasive
philosophical
pique
placate
plagiarize
polemic
precedent
precept
precipitate
precipitous
preclude
precocious
precognition
preconception
preconscious
precursor
predilection
preponderance
prescient
presumptuous
pretentious
prologue
provincial
quandary
querulous
query
quiescent
quintessential
rational
reciprocate
recourse
recur
refute
relevant
repertory
requisite
resolute

resonance
rhetoric
rubric
sacrosanct
salient
sensory
sensual
simile
socialism
speculate
spurious
statue
stature
statute
stipulate
subjective
subjugate
summary
syllogism
synecdoche
temporal
temporary
tenant
tenet
their
there
thesis
they're
tragedy
transition
trite
triumviral
triune
trivialize
trope
ubiquitous
usurious
verbatim
verification
virtual
volatile
voluble
wizen
wreak
wreck
you're
your

Rhetoric

Rhetoric: The Basics 9

Ever hear of rhetoric? Of course you have, as in, "I'm sick of all the campaign rhetoric," or this common remark, "That was a rhetorical question." These statements suggest that rhetoric means puffery or chatter or pointlessness, or a combination of all three. That's one way to define rhetoric – as a form of language that sounds exaggerated or elaborate and seems to lack substance or sincerity.

A second way to define rhetoric – the way most college composition classes approach it – is as the art of discourse, a formal way of communicating by using techniques in language that effectively persuade an audience. Try swapping out this second definition for the previous definition and read those sentences in the first paragraph again. This time, the sentence "I'm sick of all the campaign rhetoric" can mean that the speaker is tired of hearing statements that are designed to manipulate an audience, while the statement "That was a rhetorical question" can mean that the person asking the question structured the sentence to influence the audience to have a response or reaction.

Rhetoric exists in many forms. From the loftiest speech by the most influential civic leader to the simple picture of a smiling baby on a package of disposable diapers, rhetoric exists in your environment to persuade and manipulate you. Here's my short list of items I have seen during the past week where it looked or sounded like someone or something was trying to influence my reaction or response:

- A political speech
- Television ad for a new Xbox 360® video game
- Magazine article featuring five ways to increase confidence
- Cereal box with picture of heart-shaped bowl of cereal
- Direct-mail card with telephone offer and picture of family at Thanksgiving dinner
- Radio ad for great service and free phone from local radio/communications company
- Newspaper with picture of community orchestra on the cover; photo taken at a church but all the religious symbols and decorations were removed using imaging software
- News website with repeated banner ads promoting services of chiropractor and holistic healer
- A color photograph of squash soup in a cookbook
- Email with colorful artwork of printer's registration marks to announce relocation of printing company to new facility
- Telephone survey from health care provider that ended in a short message about the provider's 24-hour-ask-a-nurse service
- Fleece jacket with Ferrari® logo for sale at car show

• A television program about the resilience of Galveston, Texas, after a deadly hurricane more than a century ago.

Take a minute to list some of the items you have seen or heard lately where it sounded or looked like someone was attempting to influence you in some way.

_____

_____

_____

_____

_____

_____

_____

_____

In this consumer-oriented culture, you are bombarded with rhetoric, both verbal and visual, every time you look at or listen to media, visit a business, surf the Internet, go shopping, read a book, or read your mail. The creators of this rhetoric know what they're doing when they design an ad, write a blog entry, or compose a script for a telephone survey: they're using persuasive techniques to appeal to your senses and thought processes. They're manipulating your emotions and thoughts in an attempt to elicit a specific reaction or response. The reaction or response they want may be the purchase of a specific product or service, a request for more information, preparation of a recipe in a cookbook, refusal to support a ballot issue, or any of a thousand other responses to specific stimuli. They can determine their rhetoric's effectiveness when you react or respond in the way they hope.

A brief history of rhetoric

According to author John Henry Freese, who translated a version of Aristotle's *The Art of Rhetoric*, rhetoric has existed as an identifiable style of communication since the fifth century B.C. It emerged in Sicily as a way for exiled individuals whose homes and wealth had been confiscated by the government to reclaim their property through the courts using a specific set of oratorical rules. Two people, Corax and Tisias, wrote the early rhetoric rule books and taught others specific methods and techniques that they could use to argue their cases in the courts. Corax also wrote speeches that individuals could present on their own behalf. As interest in the art of rhetoric grew, a Greek named Gorgias who "viewed rhetoric as a means of persuasion" (Freese x) began to expand on the ideas of Corax, Tisias, and others. Gorgias wrote elaborate works; Gorgias's methods and styles may have contributed to the notion that rhetoric was nothing more than puffery. During the next hundred years or so, students of these men and others refined the elements of rhetoric – defining and categorizing oratory, argument, word choice, writing style, concluding techniques, word classification, and grammar and expanding rhetoric's importance beyond the courts into other aspects of intellectual life.

In the fourth century B.C. Greek philosopher Aristotle undertook the task of organizing all of these different perspectives and analyzing the elements and influence of rhetoric. He produced several versions of works titled *The Art of Rhetoric*. Aristotle states in *The Art of Rhetoric* that rhetoric is related to dialectic, another form of argument in which participants hold some ideas in common even when they disagree (Freese 3). Aristotle describes rhetoric as a means of debating an issue whereby the participants use proofs to support their views and persuade an audience to accept their respective arguments.

In his introduction to the 1926 translation of Aristotle's *The Art of Rhetoric,* author/translator Freese discusses proofs and their significance to the practice of rhetoric. He refers to "inartificial and artificial proofs" as the means by which an orator persuades an audience. The inartificial proofs include "laws, witnesses, contracts, torture and oaths" (Freese xxxvi). The artificial proofs include devices and techniques that appeal to the audience in three areas:

> 1) **ethical,** derived from the moral character of the speaker; 2) **emotional,** the object of which is to put the hearer into a certain frame of mind; 3) **logical,** contained in the speech itself when a real or apparent truth is demonstrated. The orator must therefore be a competent judge of virtue and character; he must have a thorough knowledge of the emotions (or passions); and he must possess the power of reasoning. This being so, rhetoric must be considered as an offshoot of dialectic and of politics (including ethics). (Freese xxxii)

These proofs or rhetorical devices are inserted in the orator's text as examples, syllogisms, enthymemes, and maxims; the orator constructs the conclusion of an argument to include the information presented as proofs (Freese xxxix-xl).

We're not going to dwell in detail on all of the topics Aristotle addressed in *The Art of Rhetoric.* That's another book (or two or three) for another time. You have more immediate business to take care of. Suffice it to say that rhetoric has been the cornerstone of English composition for a lot of years and that you need to understand the basic concepts of rhetoric in order to write college papers.

When you look specifically at your college environment, you find consumer-oriented rhetoric in advertisements, posters, student publications, and speeches. For example, the poster promoting an upcoming concert that features a photo of the band in performance is using logical rhetoric to appeal to your prior knowledge of the band and emotional rhetoric to appeal to your enthusiasm for being part of a crowd that watches the band perform. The soldier-turned-student who stands in uniform in the quad and reads the names of soldiers who have died in recent military conflicts is using logical rhetoric by presenting the soldiers' names, emotional rhetoric by associating the names with death, and ethos by wearing his military uniform, which may cause some passersby to assume that he's an authority on war or death, or both. The two-dollar pizza coupon that's printed in the student paper is using logical rhetoric by appealing to your desire to save money and emotional rhetoric by displaying a picture of a delicious-looking pizza that appeals to your sense of hunger.

Academic rhetoric is more oriented toward manipulating your thought processes with regard to the subjects you study. Academic rhetoric is found in library resources, class lectures, handouts, textbooks, discussions, and the knowledge of your instructors and professors. In your

English composition class, rhetoric may manifest itself in the topics and themes of the materials the instructor chooses for assignments, in the topics and resources you choose for your writing assignments, and in class members' beliefs and values expressed during discussions and presentations. For example, your instructor is using logical rhetoric when he assigns your class a journal article that connects several allusions to homosexuality in Richard Rodriguez's *Hunger of Memory* with the journal article author's views on queer theory. Your classmate is using emotional rhetoric when he says during a class discussion that he thinks women should be paid less than men because his mom, who is always happy, never complained about having to stay home and raise kids. When your professor assigns you to view and analyze the Holocaust-themed movies *Sophie's Choice* and *Schindler's List* for their influence on viewers, she hopes you will look for examples of logical, ethical, and emotional rhetoric in the two films.

Here's where open-mindedness can be beneficial. As you become more knowledgeable about rhetoric, you will recognize when and how you are being manipulated by information. You will be better able to analyze the devices a speaker is using to persuade you and you'll be able to decide whether the information (or the speaker, or both) is factual, truthful, deceptive, misleading, sincere, or fake. You may begin to recognize that some of your long-held attitudes and beliefs might be the result of rhetoric delivered by your friends, parents, school, or other organization, at which point you may decide to self-regulate/analyze your attitudes and beliefs further to determine what you think and believe. You may even change your mind about long-held beliefs and start thinking in a new way, retaining some beliefs, discarding others, and replacing some discarded beliefs with new ones. These revelations will not occur immediately, but they do tend to happen. Be prepared, then, as you read and view various texts for your classes, that your understanding of rhetoric combined with your critical thinking skills will help you to determine the validity and usefulness of the multitude of texts in your life.

Rhetorical appeals

Sidenote: logos means many things in Greek, including speech, theory, argument, thinking, rationale, story, and meaning.

The singular of logos is logos; the plural is logoi. A logo is a symbol that represents a business or organization.

In his discussion about the mechanisms of rhetoric that influence or persuade, Aristotle identifies three types of artificial proofs: **ethical, emotional,** and **logical.** English comp instructors like to talk about these devices as **rhetorical appeals** and may refer to them by their Greek equivalents: **ethos, pathos,** and **logos.** When you analyze an essay in class, your instructor may ask, "How does the author establish ethos in this text?" "What evidence of pathos is there in this essay?" "What examples of logos are there in this article?" Your instructor may also refer to the rhetorical appeals using terms such as *credibility* or *ethics* for ethos, *emotional* or *pathetic* for pathos, and *logic* or *factual* for logos.

These devices are called rhetorical appeals because they appeal to the audience/reader's sense of ethics, emotions, or logic. But what are they? How do you identify them in a text?

Logos/logical appeals relate most to our sense of reason and our cognitive processes – the facts we have learned, the thoughts we form. Logos evokes a thoughtful, rational response. You can identify examples of logos/logical appeals when you see these types of information in a text:

• Facts, data, and statistics
• Definitions

- Quotations from experts and scholarly sources
- Citations from authorities and experts
- Analogies based on literal, historical, and scientific sources
- Conclusions reached based on denotative language
- Opinions based on fact or reason

Pathos/pathetic appeals relate most to our feeling and intuitive sides and touch the heart. Pathos evokes an emotional response. The portions of a text that create an emotional response are most often characterized by these techniques:

- Detailed language and images
- Dramatic, colorful language
- Conclusions reached through connotative language such as symbols, implications, and inferences
- Examples of emotional situations or objects
- Narratives of emotional events
- Strong, intense descriptions
- Provocative or touching tone or style
- Symbolic words and images

Ethos/ethical appeals rely on our perceptions of an experience combined with the writer's character, attitudes, beliefs, and habits. Together, these things allow us to draw a conclusion about the **credibility and/or validity** of the text. For example, when we read an article by a scientist, we expect to find evidence of scientific work within the article: our perception – "this is a scientific article" – combines with our presumed expectations of what a scientist is – "a scientist is serious, precise, analytical, maybe a bit out of the mainstream" – so that we can evaluate whether the article **looks and sounds** like it was written by a scientist. We can establish the writer's character by researching his or her background or by analyzing the context of the writer's message. If the article is filled with slang and is sloppily written, we may be suspicious of the writer and doubt the sincerity of the author and veracity of the article. If the article is well written, mentions the scientific method, and analyzes the topic using scientific words, we are more likely to believe the writer of the article and find the content of the article more believable and/or valid. Ethos is determined in an article or essay by the reader's interpretation of some or all of these elements:

- Restrained, respectful, fair-minded presentation
- Language, vocabulary, and style appropriate for audience
- Correct grammar
- Appropriate use of supporting evidence
- Accuracy and thoroughness
- Appearance
- Establishment of authority by brand, reputation, and/or identity

The chart on the next page may help you to remember the characteristics of the rhetorical appeals.

Logos

**logical appeals,
appeals to reason**

- Facts, data, and statistics
- Definitions
- Quotations from experts and scholarly sources
- Citations from authorities and experts
- Analogies based on literal, historical, and scientific sources
- Conclusions reached based on denotative language
- Opinions based on fact or reason

Pathos

**pathetic appeals,
appeals to emotion**

- Detailed language and images
- Dramatic, colorful language
- Conclusions reached through connotative language such as symbols, implications, and inferences
- Examples of emotional situations or objects
- Narratives of emotional events
- Strong, intense descriptions
- Provocative or touching tone or style
- Symbolic words and images

Ethos

**ethical appeals,
credibility/appearance**

- Restrained, respectful, fair-minded presentation
- Language, vocabulary, and style appropriate for audience
- Correct grammar
- Appropriate use of supporting evidence
- Accuracy and thoroughness
- Appearance
- Establishment of authority by brand, reputation, and/or identity

Figure 6 This chart identifies the characteristics of the three types of rhetorical appeals.

Do writers consciously decide when and how to use the various rhetorical appeals? Yes. How can you as a writer use rhetorical appeals in your own essays and research papers to present a convincing argument? It will help if you approach the task this way: The effectiveness of rhetorical appeals within a paper, speech, or message depends a great deal on the writer's purpose and the nature of the audience that will receive the message. When you can identify these three elements – the writer (or author or speaker), the audience, and the purpose – you can select the rhetorical appeals that will most effectively influence your message.

Let's look at this example. You have gone home for the weekend. Your parents say you have to honor the midnight curfew that they set for you when you were in high school. You're a college student now. You don't want a curfew. When you have that argument with your parents about how late you can stay out with your friends, which line is going to be more persuasive: "Aw, come on, everybody else's parents let them stay out all night" (dramatic language-emotional appeal) or "Last time I was home, you let me stay out until one-thirty and there weren't any problems" (fact-logical appeal, and your own experience-ethos appeal). Unless your parents are pushovers, I'll bet they will be more persuaded by the logical and ethos appeals.

Let's look at another example where a writer has incorporated the appeals techniques within a screenplay that is supposed to depict ordinary people doing ordinary things. Director-screen-writer Quentin Tarantino has stated in interviews that he likes to tell stories about the truth in people's lives. In the opening scenes of his screenplay *Pulp Fiction,* the characters Honey Bunny (called Young Woman in the script) and Pumpkin (called Young Man in the script) are seated in a restaurant making plans to rob someplace to get money. It's obvious that they are trying to determine what sort of establishment is the most suitable to rob. Pumpkin starts taking about the ease with which banks can be robbed – because they're insured, he says – and then, after giving an example of someone he's heard about who successfully robbed a bank using a phone, compares the bank situation to the potential of other places. He says places that sell liquor are likely to have guns behind the counter – again giving an example of a possible liquor store scenario where the clerk has a gun – so they're no good. Then he observes that restaurants are probably a good choice, even if they aren't all that popular:

> Young Man (Pumpkin): People never rob restaurants. Why not? Bars, liquor stores, gas stations, you get your head blown off stickin' up one of them. Restaurants, on the other hand, you catch them with their pants down. They're not expecting to get robbed, or not as expecting. *(Pulp Fiction)*

Pumpkin then goes on to explain the advantages of robbing a restaurant – restaurants are insured, managers don't care, waitresses aren't going to try to be heroes, busboys don't care, and the customers are more concerned about eating than what's going on around them. He reminds Honey Bunny how, at the last liquor store they held up, they made more from collecting all of the customers' wallets than they did from the register. She agrees, telling him that taking the wallets was a good idea. He then brings his argument to a close by pointing out that lots of people go to restaurants and Honey Bunny draws the conclusion that there must be lots of wallets. Then she says, "Pretty smart. I'm ready, let's go, right here, right now" *(Pulp Fiction).* Even when we brush aside the relative intelligence of both characters, we can see that Pumpkin uses all sorts of facts (logical appeals) to describe the different scenarios to convince Honey Bunny that they should rob the restaurant where they are drinking coffee.

Now let's look at an example you're likely to run across in the classroom. A group of classmates is giving a presentation on the advantages of being a vegetarian. Each student has agreed to discuss a different aspect of the topic. Joe will talk about the health issues; Karen, the financial issues; Mike, the cooking issues; and Oma, the cultural and religious issues. Joe's presentation includes charts and statistics that illustrate the reduced incidence of cancer and heart disease in long-time vegetarians. Karen's presentation includes, among other things, a comparison chart that shows that it is cheaper to purchase vegetarian protein sources at three local supermarkets than it is to buy meat with the same protein levels. Mike's presentation includes cookbooks with vegetarian recipes and a discussion of the relative cost of a vegetarian and non-vegetarian

Thanksgiving meal. Oma's presentation includes several general statements about how she has always been a vegetarian, that she and her friends who were vegetarians were ridiculed at her high school, that being a vegetarian is not like being in a cult, and how she found it really difficult to find vegetarian restaurants in the little town where she used to live. She concludes her remarks with the statement, "I hate people who eat meat."

If you are considering becoming a vegetarian, whose presentation(s) offer(s) the most useful information to help you understand vegetarianism? Whose presentation(s) addresses your concerns about becoming a vegetarian? Whose presentation(s) did you find it difficult to apply to your situation? If you were going to thank any of the speakers for providing the information that most influenced your decision to become a vegetarian, who would you thank?

These are simple examples, but the general idea should be clear. While there is no set rule regarding the effectiveness of various types of rhetorical appeals in a conversation or argument, it should be evident that logic, facts, quotes from scholarly sources, a sense of authority by the speaker, and easy-to-understand information are more likely to influence the audience than vivid language and emotional pleas. College papers (and presentations) rely heavily on the presence of logical and ethics appeals to make a convincing argument because they are presented in a scholarly environment that thrives on researched evidence and the credentials of the researcher.

Convincing arguments happen when the author of the argument has a sense of understanding, or ownership, about his or her topic. If that author is you, that means you're going to have to do some research in order to acquire the necessary facts, data, and quotes to make the topic "yours" and to be able to speak or write about it with authority. It may sound easier to be convincing about a subject based on your gut feelings and memories – and that may be true when you're having a conversation with your girlfriend about your impressions of her behavior at last night's party – but it's difficult to write a convincing paper with a convincing argument if you don't know anything about the subject and all you're doing is pushing words around on paper. Besides, your professor or instructor is much more likely to enjoy reading a paper in which the argument is logically stated, the topic has been thoroughly researched, the key elements of the argument are clearly supported with documented evidence, and the conclusion is clearly stated. Papers written "from the gut" tend to be just as annoying to read as the argument would be if it were spoken. And one of your goals in college, if you haven't figured it out by now, is to keep your teachers happy long enough to earn good grades and complete their classes.

Analyzing an essay for rhetorical appeals

In this sample essay I have included examples of all three types of appeals and labeled some of the appeals by their characteristics so you can see what makes them effective. Take a look at the appeals that have been underlined but not labeled. Using the chart on page 84 as a guide, see if you can identify the types of appeals and identify the characteristic that makes the appeal effective. You can write your responses in the margins.

Traumatic brain injury affects Iraq War veterans

When U.S. Army Second Lieutenant Hank Graber began making plans to re-

turn home from Iraq in April 2008, he had hoped to return immediately to his for- ~~LOGOS~~
mer job as a maintenance mechanic at the Melbourne Mining Company outside fact
his hometown of Leadville, Colorado. Although his wife Bonnie had worked
part-time as a certified nursing assistant during his tour of duty, both she and
Hank believed that Bonnie would be happier at home, raising their two toddlers. PATHOS
example of emotional

Hank's plans changed a few months after he arrived in Leadville. Instead of situation
being the local war hero and the family's sole breadwinner, he developed frequent PATHOS
headaches, tinnitus, and muscle spasms in his extremities. By the end of August, connotative language
Hank's headaches were so frequent that he was missing at least two days of work
each week. He still had troubles with his balance, and a new problem, twitching in
his fingers and feet, was more annoying than it was painful. Bonnie had quit her
job but was looking for another one because she was afraid Hank was about to
lose his, and their mutual disappointment about Hank's health and their job situation had caused more arguments than either of them could remember.

Hank blamed himself, felt angry and frustrated much of the time, and didn't
enjoy spending time with the children. He was concerned that the medication he
was taking for his headaches was doing physical damage to his stomach. When
doctors at the VA hospital in Denver told Hank that they believed Hank was suffering from post-traumatic stress disorder (PTSD) due to the consequences of an
untreated traumatic brain injury caused by shock waves from the IED explosion,
Hank was relieved that someone had finally found a reason for his troubles.

Traumatic brain injury has become the "signature injury of soldiers in the
Iraq war," according to a recent study (Rand 3). From mild concussions to injuries
that violently shake, tear, and destroy delicate brain tissues within the skull, an increasing number of occurrences of traumatic brain injury have been attributed to
increased usage of improvised explosive devices (Rand 25). Likewise, the number
of soldiers who survive their injuries is at an all-time high.

> As of early January 2008, the Department of Defense (DoD) reports
> a total of 3,453 hostile deaths and over 30,721 wounded in action in
> Afghanistan and Iraq…. Although a high percentage of those wounded is
> returned to duty within 72 hours, a significant number of military person-
> nel are medically evacuated from theater (including approximately 30,000
> servicemembers with nonhostile injuries or other medical issues/diseases).
> Approximately 3,000 servicemembers returned home from Iraq or
> Afghanistan with severe wounds, illnesses, and/or disabilities, including
> amputations, serious burns, spinal-cord injuries, blindness, and traumatic
> brain injuries (President's Commission on Care for America's Returning
> Wounded Warriors, 2007). The ratio of wounded to killed is higher than in
> previous conflicts as a result of advances in combat medicine and body
> armor. Wounded soldiers who would have likely died in previous conflicts
> are instead saved, but with significant physical, emotional, and cognitive
> injuries. Thus, caring for these wounded often requires an intensive men-
> tal-health component in addition to traditional rehabilitation services.

LOGOS
conclusions based on denotative language

Traumatic brain injury ranges from mild to severe, with a spectrum of symptoms that includes decreased ability to concentrate, anxiety, forgetfulness, amnesia, loss of consciousness, various neurological impairments, coma, skull fractures, intercranial bleeding and death (Rand 6). Treatment depends on the severity of the injury, ranging from months to years. The more severe the injury, the more likely there will be permanent evidence of the injury in the person's physical, behavioral, and cognitive processes (Barrows 9).

Researchers at Johns Hopkins University are studying the effects of explosion shock waves on the body (Popular Science). Using models of human heads loaded with sensors, the researchers are blasting forced air at the dummy heads to determine what happens inside the skull when external pressure is applied. Other tests, including psychological and neurological tests on returning soldiers, have shown that shock waves from explosions to parts of the body besides the head have caused abnormal brain-wave patterns and altered brain-hormone levels (Popular Science). The results of this research suggest that the body responds to shock waves from a blast in a way that can cause "brain dysfunction" (Popular Science).

Other researchers are looking at the impact of electromagnetic waves that result when a bomb explodes. Using pigs wired with sensors, scientists are measuring the impact of the blast wave, electromagnetic pulse, levels of light and noise, and exposure to gases created by the explosion (Popular Science).

As researchers learn more about the effects of shock waves, they will be better able to identify ways to protect the body and brain during battle. Wearing a helmet has long been the prescribed method of protecting the head from physical injury. If research bears out, designers of military armor are going to have to consider the impact of blast pressure and electromagnetic pulses on the whole body.

For soldiers like Hank Graber, this data supports his doctors' diagnoses that his problems, initially caused by injury to his brain, extended to include the mental/emotional disorder of PTSD. The data helps Hank and other soldiers like him to realize that treatment is possible, and that recovery is not elusive. Treatment for emotional and mental disorders wasn't part of Hank's plan when he started thinking about coming home, but now that he's back in the States and treatment is available, he is wise to take advantage of the services for the sake of his own health and the well-being of his family. His wife and children have missed him.

Works Cited

Barrow Neurological Institute. *Traumatic Brain Injury Guidebook.* 2 Sept. 2008.
    <www.thebarrow.org/Medical_Specialties_Centers_and_Clinics/Neu
    rotrauma_Program/Traumatic_Brain_Injury/index.htm?ssSourceNodeId
    =5012473&ssSourceSiteId=50 12151>

Hagerman, Eric. "Shock to the System." *Popular Science.* 27 Sept. 2008.
    <http://www.popsci.com/military-aviation-%2526-space/article/2008-
    08/shock-system>

Tanielian, Terry, and Lisa H. Jaycox, Eds. *Invisible Wounds of War: Psychological and Cognitive Injuries, Their Consequences, and Services to Assist Recovery.* 27 Sept. 2008. <http://www.rand.org>

If you still have questions about how rhetorical appeals work within an essay, take another look at the chart on page 84. Imagine or recollect examples of persuasive texts you might have seen recently in a book, billboard, movie, or advertisement that contained some of the characteristics of the three types of appeals. Think about how the characteristics made the texts persuasive. For example, the advertisement for a popular children's cold medication grabs the viewer's attention with pathetic appeals (characteristic: example of emotional situation) when it opens with a sick little kid coughing and looking unhappy. A newspaper article about presidential election results relies heavily on logical appeals (characteristic: data, facts, and statistics) in an illustration of a United States map with the number of electoral votes noted in each state; it also uses pathetic appeals (characteristic: vivid imagery) by coloring various states red and blue. The cover of a new novel by John Grisham bears the author's name in a more conspicuous color than the title of the book, using ethical appeals and author credibility to persuade the consumer to buy the book because it's "another book by best-selling author John Grisham."

List some of the texts you have seen recently. Identify the category (logos, pathos, or ethos) and the characteristic within the category that makes the appeal work.

Rhetorical triangle

A page or so ago, I stated that the effectiveness of rhetorical appeals within a paper, speech, or message depends a great deal on the writer, the writer's purpose, and the nature of the audience that will receive the message. These three elements – **the writer** (also referred to as the **author** or **speaker**), **the audience, and the purpose** – are sometimes referred to as points on the **rhetorical triangle.** Your English comp professor or instructor may sketch a triangle on the board and label each of the angles and say something pithy like "This is the rhetorical triangle. Write it down. Look at it. Remember it. You need to know it." You'll stare at it, think "But it's just a triangle with fringies," and then let your brain wander to more exciting subjects.

The rhetorical triangle is indeed just a triangle, but it's also a symbol, and symbols are important. It's also one of the few math symbols and signs you're going to see in English comp class, and that in itself makes it exciting. The rhetorical triangle looks like this:

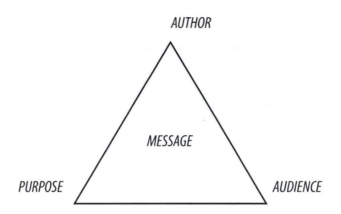

Figure 7 The elements author, audience, and purpose influence the overall message. This concept is referred to as the rhetorical triangle.

When you write a paper, you should think about how the knowledge you have as the author combines with the purpose of your paper and your anticipated audience to influence your message. If you are knowledgeable about your subject, and the intended purpose of your paper is to demonstrate your knowledge about the subject to your professor, then you will write your paper in such a way that your knowledge will be evident and your professor will be able to relate to its content. That means you will use the format or style your professor requires, and you will stay on topic from start to finish so that your presentation is organized and easy to understand. Your tone will be academic rather than informal. The types of rhetorical appeals you use in your paper will be influenced by **your understanding of the topic (author), the point you**

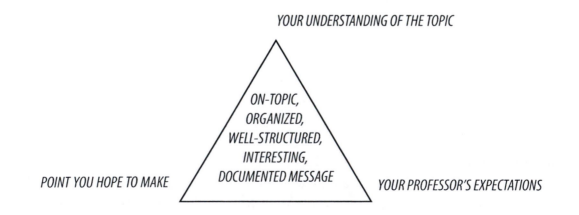

Figure 8 These interpretations of author, audience, and purpose illustrate the process that occurs when you write an essay or research paper to fulfill an assignment.

hope to make (purpose of your paper), and your professor's expectations (audience). When you write a paper, you can control these things so that your message is as clear as it can be.

Likewise, when you read a text, you should look for information that identifies author, audience, and purpose. Knowing these things will help you to better understand the message of the text. The chart below contains a list of tips that will help you analyze a verbal or visual text for author, audience, and purpose. You may want to use this information as a checklist or short-answer sheet when you do a critical reading of texts that you need to analyze rhetorically.

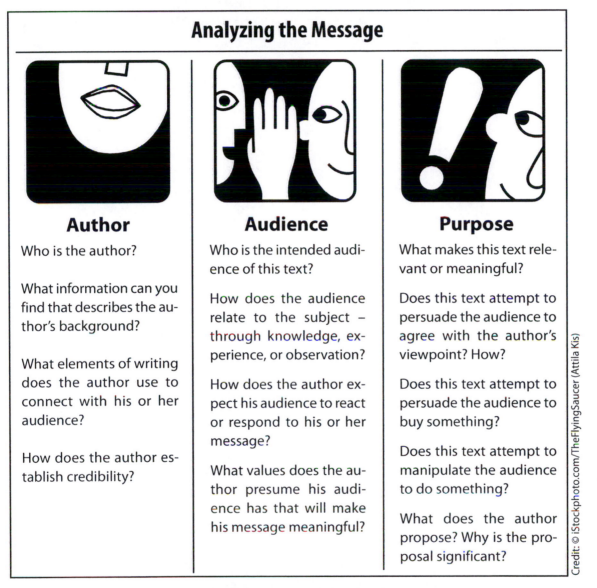

Analyzing the Message

Author

Who is the author?

What information can you find that describes the author's background?

What elements of writing does the author use to connect with his or her audience?

How does the author establish credibility?

Audience

Who is the intended audience of this text?

How does the audience relate to the subject – through knowledge, experience, or observation?

How does the author expect his audience to react or respond to his or her message?

What values does the author presume his audience has that will make his message meaningful?

Purpose

What makes this text relevant or meaningful?

Does this text attempt to persuade the audience to agree with the author's viewpoint? How?

Does this text attempt to persuade the audience to buy something?

Does this text attempt to manipulate the audience to do something?

What does the author propose? Why is the proposal significant?

Credit: © iStockphoto.com/TheFlyingSaucer (Attila Kis)

Figure 9 The answers to these questions will help you develop a rhetorical analysis of a specific text.

Analyzing a text rhetorically means scrutinizing a verbal or visual text for clues about its persuasiveness. When you "do a rhetorical analysis of a text," you are expected to identify, interpret, analyze, evaluate, infer, and explain the functions of the author, audience, and purpose of the text on the text's overall message. You are also expected to identify, interpret, analyze, evaluate, infer, and explain the way the three types of rhetorical appeals (logos, pathos, and ethos) function within a text so you can explain how the rhetorical appeals persuade or influence the reader. You also need to analyze the style and structure of the text, looking at elements such as word choice, fluency, point of view, tone, and so on. Rhetorical analysis is not a black-and-white, right-or-wrong process. How you interpret a text depends on your knowledge and experience about the topic of the text, as well as your viewpoint of the text. The more you understand rhetoric and the more you know about a topic of a text, the richer your rhetorical analysis of that text will be.

In Chapter 10, you will be analyzing verbal and visual texts rhetorically. In Chapter 15, you will find information about writing a rhetorical analysis essay. Remember the concepts of the rhetorical appeals and the rhetorical triangle. You will need them to understand the content of these two chapters.

Analyzing Verbal and Visual Rhetoric **10**

Rhetorical analysis is an activity that's done in many English comp classes. You may be asked to analyze an article for its rhetorical techniques, or you may have to analyze an advertisement, a photo, media program, or other visual text for its rhetorical appeals. Occasionally, an instructor or professor will send you out into the community to analyze an environment such as a business, park, institution, or residence.

In this chapter you will find an essay and several advertisements that you can use to practice your rhetorical analysis skills. Portions of the essays and images have notations to help you better understand the concept of rhetorical analysis. Please complete the rhetorical analysis of each essay and image and write a conclusion about the overall impact and effectiveness of the rhetorical appeals you have found. Writing your responses will help you organize your ideas.

Analyzing an essay

This essay is the prologue of the book, *Channels of Desire,* written in 1982 by Stuart and Elizabeth Ewen. The Ewens are professors: Stuart Ewen teaches in the Department of Film and Media Studies at Hunter College and in the Ph.D. Programs in History, Sociology, and American Studies at the City University of New York Graduate Center (New York University). Elizabeth Ewen is a professor of American Studies at the State University of New York (BarnesandNoble.com). The two have co-authored books about media studies and American culture.

Each of the vignettes in the prologue is designed to show how some element of contemporary society influences the individual through various logical, pathetic, and ethical appeals. As you read though each vignette, identify the logical, pathetic, and/or ethical appeals that influence action within each scene or setting. Pay close attention to other rhetorical techniques such as word choice, language style, tone, voice, and style that help the Ewens build their case that patterns exist in overwhelming abundance in today's world.

In the Shadow of the Image

By Stuart and Elizabeth Ewen

Maria Aguilar was born twenty-seven years ago near Mayaguez, on the island of Puerto Rico. Her family had lived off the land for generations. Today she sits in a rattling IRT subway car, speeding through the iron and rock guts of Manhattan. She sits on the train, her ears dazed by the loud outcry of wheels against tracks. Surrounded by a galaxy of unknown fellow strangers, she looks up at a long strip of colorful signboards placed high above the bobbing heads of the others. All the posters call for her attention. Looking down at her, a blond-haired lady cabdriver leans out of her driver's side window. Here is the famed philosopher of this strange urban world, and a woman she can talk to. The tough-wise eyes of the cabby combined with a youthful beauty, speaking to Maria Aguilar directly: *"Estoy sentada 12 horas al dia. Lo ultimo que necesito son hemorroides."* (I sit for twelve hours a day. The last thing I need are hemorrhoids.) Under this candid testimonial lies a package of Preparation H ointment, and the promise *"Alivia dolores y picasonas. Y ayuda a reducir la hinchazon."* (Relieves pain and itching. And helps reduce swelling.) As her mind's eye takes it all in, the train sweeps into Maria's stop. She gets out; climbs the stairs to the street; walks to work where she will spend her day sitting on a stool in a small garment factory, sewing hems on pretty dresses.

LOGOS
quote from expert
(could also be ETHOS)

Every day, while Benny Doyle drives his Mustang to work along State Road Number 20, he passes a giant billboard along the shoulder. The billboard is selling whiskey and features a woman in a black velvet dress stretching across its brilliant canvas. As Benny Doyle downshifts by, the lounging beauty looks out to him. Day after day he sees her here. The first time he wasn't sure, but now he's convinced that her eyes are following him.

The morning sun shines on the red-tan forehead of Bill O'Conner as he drinks espresso on his sun deck, alongside the ocean cliffs of La Jolla, California. Turning through the daily paper, he reads a story about Zimbabwe. "Rhodesia," he thinks to himself. The story argues that a large number of Africans in Zimbabwe are fearful about black majority rule, and are concerned over, a white exodus. Two black hotel workers are quoted by the article. Bill puts this, as a fact, into his mind. Later that day, over a business lunch, he repeats the story to five white business associates, sitting at the restaurant table. They share a superior laugh over the ineptitude of black African political rule. Three more tellings, children, of the first, take place over the next four days. These are spoken by two of Bill O'Conner's luncheon companions; passed on to still others in the supposed voice of political wisdom.

Barbara and John Marsh get into their seven-year-old Dodge pickup and drive twenty-three miles to the nearest Sears in Cedar Rapids. After years of breakdowns and months of hesitation they've decided to buy a new washing machine. They come to Sears because it is there, and because they believe that their new Sears machine will be steady and reliable. The Marshes will pay for their purchase for the next year or so.

Barbara's great-grandfather, Elijah Simmons, had purchased a cream-separator from Sears, Roebuck in 1897 and…

When the clock-radio sprang the morning affront upon him, Archie Bishop rolled resentfully out of his crumpled bed and trudged slowly to the John. A few moments later he was unconsciously squeezing toothpaste out of a mess of red and white Colgate packaging. A dozen scrubs of the mouth and he expectorated a white, minty glob into the basin. Still groggy, he turned on the hot water, slapping occasional palmfuls onto his gray face. A can of Noxzema shave cream sat on the edge of the sink, a film of crud and whiskers across its once neat label. Archie reached for the bomb and filled his left hand with a white creamy mound, then spread it over his beard. He shaved, then looked with resignation at the regular collection of cuts on his neck. Stepping into a shower, he soaped up with a soap that promised to wake him up. Groggily, he then grabbed a bottle of Clairol Herbal Essence Shampoo. He turned the tablet-shaped bottle to its back label, carefully reading the "Directions." "Wet hair." He wet his hair. "Lather." He lathered. "Rinse." He rinsed. "Repeat if necessary." Not sure whether it was altogether necessary, he repeated the process according to the directions.

Late in the evening, Maria Aguilar stepped back in the subway train, heading home to the Bronx after a long and tiring day. This time, a poster told her that "The Pain Stops Here!" She barely noticed, but later she would swallow two New Extra Strength Bufferin tablets with a glass of water from a rusty tap.

Two cockroaches in cartoon form leer out onto the street from a wall advertisement. The man cockroach is drawn like a hipster, wearing shades and a cockroach zoot-suit. He strolls hand-in-hand with a lady cockroach, who is dressed like a floozy and blushing beet-red. Caught in the midst of their cockroach-rendezvous, they step sinfully into a Black Flag Roach Motel. Beneath them in Spanish, the words: *Las Cucarachas entran, pero non pueden salir.* (In the English version: Cockroaches check in, but they don't check out.) The roaches are trapped; sin is punished. Salvation is gauged by one's ability to live roach-free. The sinners of the earth shall be inundated by roaches. Moral tales and insects encourage passersby to rid their houses of sin. In their homes, sometimes, people wonder whether God has forsaken them.

PATHOS
Conclusion reached through connotative language/symbol

Beverly Jackson sits at a metal and tan Formica table and looks through the *New York Post.* She is bombarded by a catalog of horror. Children are mutilated… subway riders attacked. Fanatics are marauding and noble despots lie in bloody heaps. Occasionally someone steps off the crime-infested streets to claim a million dollars in lottery winnings. Beverly Jackson's skin crawls; she feels a knot encircling her lungs. She is beset by immobility, hopelessness, depression. Slowly she walks over to her sixth-floor window, gazing out into the sooty afternoon. From the empty street below, Beverly Jackson imagines a crowd yelling "Jump!.. Jump!"

PATHOS
Symbolic words/images

Between 1957 and 1966 Frank Miller saw <u>a dozen John Wayne movies, countless other westerns, and war dramas.</u> In 1969 he led a charge up a hill without a name in Southeast Asia. No one followed; he took a bullet in the chest. Today he sits in a chair and doesn't get up. He feels that images betrayed him, and now he <u>camps out across from the White House while another movie star cuts benefits for veterans.</u> In the morning newspaper he reads of a massive weapons buildup taking place....

Gina Concepcion now comes to school wearing the Jordache look. All this has been made possible by weeks and weeks of afterschool employment at a supermarket checkout counter. Now, each morning, she tugs the decorative denim over her young legs, sucking in her lean belly to close the snaps. <u>These pants are expensive compared to the "no-name" brands, but they're worth it, she reasons.</u> They fit better, and she fits better.

It was ten in the morning and Joyce Hopkins stood before a mirror next to her bed. Her interview at General Public Utilities, Nuclear Division was only four hours away and all she could think was "What to wear?" A half-hour later Joyce stood again before the mirror, wearing a slip and stockings. On the bed, next to her, lay a two-foot-mountain of discarded options. <u>Mocking the title of a recent bestseller, which she hadn't read, she said aloud to herself, "Dress for Success— What do they like?"</u> At one o'clock she walked out the door wearing a brownish tweed jacket; a cream-colored <u>Qiana blouse,</u> full-cut with a tied collar; a dark beige skirt, fairly straight and hemmed (by Maria Aguilar) two inches below the knee; shear fawn stockings, and simple but elegant reddish-brown pumps on her feet. Her hair was to the shoulder, her look tawny. When she got the job she thanked her friend Millie, a middle manager, for the tip not to wear pants.

Joe Davis stood at the endless conveyor, placing caps on a round-the-clock parade of automobile radiators. His nose and eyes burned. His ears buzzed in the din. In a furtive moment he looked up and to the right. On the plant wall was <u>a large yellow sign with THINK! printed on it</u> in bold type. Joe turned back quickly to the radiator caps. Fifty years earlier in another factory, in another state, <u>Joe's grandfather, Nat Davis, had looked up and seen another sign: A Clean Machine Runs Better. Your Body Is a Machine. KEEP IT CLEAN.</u> Though he tried and tried, Joe Davis' grandfather was never able to get the dirt out from under his nails. Neither could his great-grandfather, who couldn't read.

In 1952 Mary Bird left her family in Charleston to earn money as a maid in a Philadelphia suburb. She earned thirty-five dollars a week, plus room and board, in a dingy retreat of a ranch-style tract house. Twenty-eight years later she sits on a bus, heading toward her small room in north Philly. Across from her, on an advertising poster, a sumptuous meal is displayed. <u>Golden fried chicken, green beans glistening with butter and flecked by pimento, and a fluffy cloud of rice fill the greater part of a calico-patterned dinner plate. Next to the plate sits a steaming boat of gravy, and an icy drink in an amber tumbler.</u> The plate is on a quilted blue placemat, flanked by a thick linen napkin and colonial silverware. As Mary Bird's hungers are aroused, the wording on the placard instructs her: "Come home to Carolina."

Shopping List
paper towels
milk
eggs
"rice crispies"
snacks for kids (twinkies, chips, etc.)
potatoes
coke, ginger ale, plain soda
cheer
brillo
peanut butter
bread
ragu (2 jars)
spaghetti
saran wrap
salad
get cleaning, bank, must pay electric!!!

PATHOS
Symbolic word/image
(could also be ETHOS)

On his way to Nina's house, Sidney passed an ad for Smirnoff vodka. <u>A sultry beauty with wet hair and beads of moisture on her smooth, tanned face looked out at him. "Try a Main Squeeze."</u> For a teenage boy the invitation transcended the arena of drink; he felt a quick throb-pulse at the base of his belly and his step quickened.

In October of 1957, at the age of two and a half, Aaron Stone was watching television. Suddenly, from the black screen, there leaped a <u>circus clown, selling children's vitamins</u> and yelling "Hi! boys and girls!" He ran, terrified, from the room, screaming. For years after, Aaron watched television in perpetual fear that the <u>vitamin clown</u> would reappear. Slowly his family assured him that the television was just a mechanical box and couldn't really hurt him, that the vitamin clown was harmless. Today, as an adult, Aaron Stone takes vitamins, is ambivalent about clowns, and watches television, although there are occasional moments of anxiety.

These are some of the facts of our lives; disparate moments, disconnected, dissociated. Meaningless moments. Random incidents. Memory traces. Each is an unplanned encounter, part of day-to-day existence. Viewed alone, each by itself, such spaces of our lives seem insignificant, trivial. They are the decisions and reveries of survival; the stuff of small talk; the chance preoccupations of our eyes and minds in a world of images—soon forgotten.

Viewed together, however, as an ensemble, an integrated panorama of social life, human activity, hope and despair, images and information, another tale unfolds from these vignettes. They reveal a pattern of life, the structures of perception.

As familiar moments in American life, all of these events bear the footprints of a history that weighs upon us, but is largely untold. <u>We live and breathe an atmosphere where mass images are everywhere in evidence: mass produced mass distributed. In the streets in our homes, among a crowd, or alone, they speak to us, overwhelm our vision.</u>

Their presence, their messages are given; unavoidable. Though their history is still relatively short, their prehistory is, for the most part, forgotten, unimaginable.

The history that unites the seemingly random routines of daily life is one that embraces the rise of an industrial consumer society. It involves explosive interactions between modernity and old ways of life. It includes the proliferation, over days and decades, of a wide, repeatable vernacular of commercial images and ideas. This history spells new patterns of social, productive, and political life.

Rhetorical analysis of "In the Shadow of the Image"

1) What types of rhetorical appeals did you find in the essay?

_____

_____

_____

_____

_____

_____

2) List a couple of examples of each type of appeal.

_____

_____

_____

_____

_____

_____

_____

_____

3) How did the appeals influence your reaction to the essay's content?

_____

_____

_____

_____

4) Who is the assumed audience of this text?

_____

_____

_____

5) Do the writers succeed or fail in reaching their audience? Why?

_____

_____

_____

Analyzing visual text

Advertisements are designed using rhetorical appeals to stimulate the viewer to do something that involves the item or activity in the ad. The rhetorical appeals may be logical, pathetic, or ethical, or any combination of the three. The "call to action" may be obvious: to purchase the advertised product or service, send a letter to a congressman, vote on a ballot issue, request more information, watch a program, or use the services of the company presenting the ad. Or the overall message in the ad may be subtle or implied.

The guide on page 100 contains points to consider as you analyze the ads on the following pages. Use your critical thinking skills to interpret, analyze, evaluate, infer, and explain your opinions. Keep in mind that there are no right or wrong answers when you interpret visual texts for rhetoric. Your interpretation depends on your vantage point, knowledge, and experience.

Guide for Analyzing Visual Texts for Rhetoric

1. Describe the nature of the pictures and words within the visual text you're analyzing.

2. What activity is occurring in the visual text?

3. If the visual text is an ad, what is the call to action? What does the ad want you to do?

4. If the visual text is a photograph or other creative work, what is the overall idea it presents?

5. When you look at the visual text, do you get a sense of balance? Do the elements seem centered or off-centered? What impact does placement of the elements have on your response to the visual text?

6. White space is the open area (without words or images) within a visual text. If the text has white space, how does that space influence your reaction to it?

7. If the visual text is an ad, is there verbal text to support the photographs and convey a message? Too much text? Not enough? Too many photos? Not enough? Does the verbal text function denotatively or connotatively?

8. What is the significance of signs and symbols in the visual text?

9. How do the physical features (species, hair color, age, gender, ethnicity, expression, relationships) of living things in the visual text convey a particular idea or message?

10. How do the physical characteristics (size, shape, color, surface texture) of non-living things convey a particular idea or message?

11. How does the visual text create a mood?

12. How do lighting and colors affect your response to the visual text?

13. What is the theme of the visual text?

14. What message does the visual text convey about culture and society?

WE GET YOU THERE.

nationwise
car rental

1-800-AUTOREADY

The fine print reads "Advance reservations required. Leasing special offers subject to local, state, and federal laws without consideration to provisions and policies of Nationwise Corp. and its subsidiaries. Leasing services restricted to persons 25 and older with a valid drivers license at the time of lease. Cancellations less than 48 hours in advance subject to penalty. Proof of insurance required on all vehicle leases. All leases subject to availability. One-way rentals include 40% surcharge for return to point of origin. All rentals subject to refueling fee of $50 plus price of fuel."

sable
SHOW YOUR TRUE COLORS

The fine print reads "Foundation-Ivory Glow; Eye Shadow-Shimmer Ice; Mascara-Satin Black; Eyeliner-Plum Passion; Lip Gloss-Plum Tart"

The fine print reads "Camisole, 100% silk, deep chocolate, $234"

Credit: © Crestock.com/zdenkamicka (Zdenka Micka)

NO FEAR
tales of bravery
starts Wednesday on the DRAMA network

Credit: © iStockphoto.com/DanielBendjy (Daniel Bendjy)

Logical Fallacies: The Basics **11**

If rhetorical appeals are the means by which a writer persuades an audience to accept his or her claim by using facts, emotional language, and the writer's character and values, then logical fallacies represent flaws in the writer's reasoning in an attempt to further influence the audience.

You have certainly had conversations where your counterpart in the discussion said something that didn't make sense, stretched an idea, or bounced suddenly from one point to another. You might have reacted by saying, "Didn't you just sort of skip over the real issue?" or "That's stretching things a lot" or "You lost me on that line of reasoning" or something similar. That's essentially what happens when a logical fallacy is used in an argument: the reasoning/logic stops making sense, which renders the argument invalid or its conclusion incorrect.

A logical fallacy is a flaw or mistake in reasoning that makes the argument invalid or its conclusion incorrect. Logical fallacies, on the whole, represent distorted logic. They distort the truth or prevent the audience from arriving at a conclusion and discovering the truth. Sometimes the distortion is deliberately deceptive; other times, the distortions occur as a result of lack of information. Rhetorical techniques that rely predominantly on emotion or ethos rather than fact create the basis of many logical fallacies. Writers of papers for English comp class often use fallacies as a way to expedite an argument or gloss over the lack of supporting evidence an argument needs. Sometimes the fallacies they use have been passed along from parent to child, sibling to sibling, teacher to student, authority figure to subordinate, or idol to fan; the student has accepted a theory or idea from someone without investigating its validity or truth.

Aristotle divided fallacies into three categories: fallacies of relevance, fallacies of ambiguity, and fallacies of presumption (Logical Fallacies.info). Writers use **fallacies of relevance to propose information that doesn't have any bearing on the truth.** They use **fallacies of ambiguity to manipulate language to deceive the audience.** Writers base **fallacies of presumption on false information, which prevents the audience from reaching a logical conclusion.** An additional category, **component fallacies,** should be added to this list. **Component fallacies occur when a writer does not establish a clear connection between facts or ideas he or she identifies in the argument.**

On the next several pages are descriptions and examples of the more common logical fallacies. As you read through the list, think about situations where you might have heard or experienced the fallacy. In the margins, jot down examples that will help jog your memory. Listen to conversations and dialogues, such as classroom discussions and news presentations, where logical fallacies are used to persuade the audience. Pay close attention to your own statements to determine if you rely on logical fallacies or the truth to persuade others. As you read and write, be aware of the use of fallacies to bolster an argument or deflect attention away from a significant point.

Fallacies of relevance

Ad hominem, or Personal Attack – the argument attacks or criticizes some aspect of the individual or group supporting an idea, rather than attacking the idea itself, in order to discredit the idea.

> *EXAMPLE:* "Gary Johnson is a 'young earth creationist' who says that carbon-dating tests are part of a conspiracy to conceal the fact that the earth is only a few thousand years old. Gary Johnson dropped out of school after the eighth grade. Therefore, carbon-dating tests prove that the earth must be millions of years old." *(This ad hominem attack criticizes Gary Johnson's education but does not challenge his idea.)*

Bandwagon Fallacy – the notion that because more and more people accept an idea or follow a trend, then the idea or trend must be valid.

> *EXAMPLE:* "Many of the students at Whitman High School started drinking diet soda with mashed banana added to it because a teacher said it was a way to lose weight. Nobody recalls who the teacher was, and now the students at Camino Real, Casper, and Roosevelt high schools are also drinking the soda-banana mixture as a diet drink. Judging from the drink's popularity, that must mean that it works." *(There is no medical or scientific evidence that the mixture works, but its popularity implies that it has medical or scientific merit.)*

Gambler's Fallacy – the notion that the probability of an occurrence is based on past results rather than the properties of the activity.

> *EXAMPLE:* "Because the last three employees hired for the job have quit abruptly after two months, the new employee hired for the job will also quit after two months." *(While there is a pattern of people leaving the specific job, there is no apparent connection between the skills and personality of the new employee and the departures of the previous employees.)*

Genetic Fallacy – the notion that someone or something must be inferior due to ethnicity, geographical origin, or race.

> *EXAMPLE:* "Everybody knows that fashion designs from Los Angeles are going to look skanky; Los Angeles is skanky." *(This is stereotyping and has no basis in fact.)*

Appeal to Authority – a type of irrelevant appeal that suggests that because someone prominent or significant supports an idea, the idea is a good one.

> *EXAMPLE:* "Because George Bush has endorsed the use of carbon-fiber prosthetics like those worn by sprinter Oscar Pistorius, every Olympic runner should be allowed to wear the devices." *(Such an endorsement has little weight because Bush has no apparent association with or expertise in the development and use of carbon-fiber prosthetics for sports activities.)*

Appeal to Consequences – a type of irrelevant appeal that suggests that having a certain belief should have pleasant or appealing consequences, or that not having a certain belief will have unpleasant or unappealing consequences.

> *EXAMPLE:* "When you support the March of Times, which is a good cause, everybody will think you are a great person. If you don't contribute, people will hate you." *(There is no way to determine if every person on the planet will be pleased if one person contributes to the charitable organization or displeased if a person does not make a donation.)*

Appeal to Pity – a type of irrelevant appeal that uses sympathy rather than reason.

> *EXAMPLE:* "Your generous donation to the Children's Assistance Fund will make a difference in a child's life." *(This kind of plea, usually accompanied by pictures of insect-infested food and children in tattered clothing, motivates the contributor to feel sorry for the child. The ad implies but does not state exactly how the donation will be used to make a difference.)*

Appeal to Tradition – the notion that older ideas and actions are better because they have been accepted as valid over time.

> *EXAMPLE:* "Organic farming as a popular technique for hobbyists has not been around as long as traditional farming; hence, traditional farming is better." *(Organic farming has been around for a long time but the implication is that it is a modern practice because it has received media attention in recent years. The statement suggests that, as a more recently identified practice, organic farming has not been as thoroughly tested and is therefore not as good as traditional farming.)*

Appeal to Force – the notion that a person's reluctance to accept an idea will have dangerous consequences from external means.

> *EXAMPLE:* "So far, all the non-believers who have stayed overnight in the house where the murders took place have developed brain cancer, leukemia, and tuberculosis. The believers are all healthy. Anyone who plans to stay in the house should be a believer." *(The threat of serious illness associated with the lack of belief in ghosts is intended to pressure a person into believing in ghosts in order to stay healthy.)*

Appeal to Novelty – the notion that because an idea is new, it is valid or true.

> *EXAMPLE:* "Because scientists have only recently discovered the similarities between dinosaurs with feathers and modern birds, the theory that birds evolved from dinosaurs must be true." *(Researchers are trying to determine the relationship between dinosaurs, flightless birds in the Mesozoic era, and modern birds. There has not been sufficient time for researchers to establish the relationship, nor have there been many detractors to tear down the scientists' hypotheses.)*

Appeal to Popularity – the notion that because an idea has received a lot of attention and popularity over time, it is a true idea.

> *EXAMPLE:* "Children that grow up in single-parent households will likely turn into

criminals before they reach middle age, while children that grow up in two-parent households will not have behavioral problems that lead to criminal activity." *(Researchers have questioned the validity of this statement but its popularity persists as a way to discourage divorce and/or criticize single parenthood.)*

Appeal to Poverty – the notion that an idea is valid or true because it is held by the poor.

EXAMPLE: "Picking up a penny and carrying the coin in your shoe will bring you good luck." *(The implication is that wealth is associated with luck, even when there is no substantiation for such a claim.)*

Appeal to Wealth – the notion that because something has more monetary value, it is the better or truer item.

EXAMPLE: "A BMW sedan costs more than a Nissan, and so the BMW is the better car." *(The premise that one car is better than another based solely on cost is not a reliable determination; the way the cars operate should also be evaluated.)*

Component Fallacies

Moralistic Fallacy – The notion that because a situation should be a certain way, it *is* that way.

EXAMPLE: "Because all American children between the ages of 6 and 16 are required to attend school, every child in the United States is smart and adept." *(This premise does not take into account the quality of education in specific school systems, absent children, home-schooled children, children that don't pay attention in school, children with learning disabilities, children whose situations prevent them from going to school, and so on.)*

Naturalistic Fallacy – The notion that because a situation is a certain way, it *should* be that way.

EXAMPLE: "Lots of kids drink alcohol before they reach their 21st birthday. Therefore, the law should be changed to make it legal for people 15 years and older to drink alcohol." *(This premise overlooks the percentages of underage drinkers and the consequences of underage drinking.)*

Red Herring – a method of using an unrelated idea to shift the focus from one topic to another.

EXAMPLE: "Driving after smoking marijuana does not endanger lives. If it did, all the head shops and convenience stores in Midtown would have gone out of business by now." *(By implying that head shops and convenience stores in Midtown depend on business from customers under the influence of marijuana, the writer has shifted the premise from heavy machinery operation while under the influence to the success of various business operations.)*

Hasty Generalization – The notion of drawing a conclusion based on incomplete evidence.

EXAMPLE: "If every low-income family in a particular city includes at least one person on disability, then every family that has at least one person on disability must be a low-income family." *(This premise is flawed because it does not take into account that disability is not related to income level or that the presence of disability has the potential to influence income.)*

Straw Man Fallacy – the notion of simplification of an argument by exaggerating or over-simplifying the argument and ignoring the details.

EXAMPLE: "The Internet is evil because it has pornography websites." *(This premise overlooks the millions of non-pornographic websites that offer educational resources, databases, and learning services.)*

Circular Reasoning – the practice of restating an idea as a premise and then a conclusion without providing evidence to prove the validity of the idea.

EXAMPLE: "American citizens enjoy the right to bear arms because the Constitution allows for it. Therefore, the government makes it possible through the highest law in the land for people to own and use guns." *(The idea in the first sentence sounds plausible, but there is nothing here that supports the idea; the second sentence is a restatement of the first.)*

Begging the Question – the practice of presenting a premise or thesis, ignoring the deeper issues of the premise, and leaping to a conclusion.

EXAMPLE: "The nation's desire for a national health care program could have a negative impact on the insurance industry, which has been overcharging consumers for decades. Because so many people need care and treatment, the government should pay for health care services by taxing the products that make people sick." *(The issue of how to deal with the insurance industry is raised and then immediately dropped, leaving the reader to speculate about its role in national health care.)*

False Cause – the practice of tying the wrong cause to an event, or suggesting that because one event occurred before the second event, that the first event must have caused the second event.

EXAMPLE: "Volcanic eruptions can alter the weather patterns in the area around the volcano. A number of volcanoes erupted around the middle of the 20th century. Not long after that, the amount of carbon dioxide in the earth's atmosphere increased exponentially, causing the phenomenon known as global warming. Therefore, volcanic eruptions are the cause of global warming." *(Many factors may have contributed to global warming. To attribute its occurrence only to volcanic eruptions is misleading and inaccurate.)*

Slippery Slope – the notion that one situation will lead to another situation that appears unrelated and that nothing can be done to prevent the situations from occurring consecutively.

EXAMPLE: "If we let the high school students grow mustaches, things will snowball. Pretty soon the kids will all have long hair and be anarchists and they'll blow up the school." *(There is no direct relationship between facial hair and anarchy or facial hair and explosions.)*

Non-sequitur – the practice of developing a conclusion that is not based on any of the premises in an argument; this is sometimes described as "the logic doesn't follow."

EXAMPLE: "The airplanes that crashed into the World Trade Center towers were hijacked by Al-Qaida extremists. There are Al-Qaida extremists in Afghanistan. Therefore, the United States should attack Iraq and bring down Saddam Hussein." *(The premises of this theory – Al-Qaida extremists and Afghanistan – are not related to the items Iraq and Saddam Hussein mentioned in the conclusion.)*

Either/Or – the notion that there are only two possible outcomes to any scenario when in fact there may be many.

EXAMPLE: "If Mexican citizens continue to enter the United States illegally, the United States as we know it will cease to exist." *(There is no substantiation for this generalization.)*

Faulty Analogy – the practice of making poor comparisons that don't make sense.

EXAMPLE: "Friendship is like a flower: fragile, short lived and subject to shattering if it isn't cared for. Therefore, people should avoid having friends." *(This comparison of flowers to friendship does not take into account that friends are human and have many attributes that flowers don't have.)*

Fallacies of Omission

Stacking the Deck – the practice of disregarding opposing points of view or evidence and only using evidence that supports a premise.

EXAMPLE: "Nothing of note has emerged from Holland in the past five hundred years except for the recent decriminalization of marijuana." *(This is not a true statement. Holland is, among other things, the source of artwork by well-known artists, unique architecture, popular tulips, and novel footwear.)*

Appeal to a Lack of Evidence – the practice of claiming that something is true because it cannot be disproved.

EXAMPLE: "Until somebody proves that God exists, He doesn't." *(This claim consists of two contradictory phrases, neither of which lends evidence to prove itself true or false.)*

Complex or Loaded Question – The practice of phrasing a statement to suggest that another, implied statement is true. These questions have an accusatory or critical tone.

EXAMPLE: The classic question, "When did you stop beating your wife?" is a loaded question because it implies that the person who is being asked the question was at some time beating his wife.

Contradictory Premise – the practice of challenging one's premise with a premise that disagrees or contradicts.

EXAMPLE: "If the government's obligation to its citizens is to protect them at all costs, then the president has to send its soldiers to war to protect the country's citizens." *(By putting one group – the soldiers – in harm's way, the government is not protecting its citizens at all costs.)*

Fallacies of Ambiguity

Fallacy of Composition – the notion that everyone in a group is capable of doing what one person can do, with the same consequences.

> *EXAMPLE:* "If one man can drink and drive on the freeway without getting into an accident, then everybody can drink and drive on the freeway without getting into an accident." *(It's feasible that one drunk driver will cause other drivers to be more careful and get out of the drunk driver's way to avoid his recklessness, but many drunk drivers on the same road may not have the capacity to maneuver around a lot of reckless driving.)*

Fallacy of Division – the notion that each part of a whole has the same character or quality as the whole.

> *EXAMPLE:* "Schools in this state have a reputation for being under-funded, which must mean that the students don't have enough resources and are therefore stupid." *(The intellectual level of each student is not wholly dependent on school funding, which makes this statement untrue.)*

Occam's Razor is a principle of logic that states that the simpler of two theories about the same situation or concept is more likely to be correct. In other words, if Theory 1 posits that it is possible to accomplish a task in two steps and Theory 2 posits that the same task can be accomplished in two steps as long as the moon is full and the person performing the task is wearing red pants and does his work in a room without windows, it is more reasonable to assume that Theory 1 is correct – that the task can be accomplished in two steps without additional conditions. Occam's razor is often used to reduce an argument to its essential elements. It is not always reliable; sometimes the complications of an argument establish the argument's validity.

Logical fallacies can be the result of sloppy or rushed research and writing. Avoid simplifying an argument and constructing a logical fallacy for the sake of introducing your thesis or claim quickly or conveniently. As you write your assignments, ask yourself whether the reasoning you are using to support your claims and ideas is sound reasoning or flawed reasoning. If it's sound, it should hold up to this challenge question: "What am I overlooking that can punch holes in my line of reasoning?" If it's flawed, it will not hold up to the same challenge question; you should be able to identify problems or distortions with your thinking.

College Writing

Essay and Thesis Statement Development **12**

Let's talk about essays. When you write a paper or an essay for English comp class, or any other class, for that matter, there are several ways you can do it. **Common essay types include the reflective, narrative, rhetorical analysis, literary analysis, synthesis, informative, and argument (or argumentative).**

Each essay type has a unique style and purpose. *Reflective essays* are personal narratives about an event or experience, the purpose of which is to reveal the writer's opinions and growth or development as a result of the experience. The *narrative essay* is a personal form of writing that tells a story; it is similar to the reflective essay. *Rhetorical analysis essays* interpret and analyze style and rhetorical techniques within a text. *Literary analysis essays* interpret and analyze literary techniques within a literary text. *Synthesis essays* draw on information from two or more sources to develop a new claim that can be supported with evidence from the sources; they form the overarching structure for the informative, argumentative, and literary analysis essays. *Informative essays* are organized in various ways, including cause-and-effect, descriptive, comparison-contrast, classification, definition, and explaining a process. Their purpose is to provide information that will enlighten an audience. *Argument* or *argumentative* essays are often referred to as research papers, critical essays, or persuasive essays and are based on gathered evidence from multiple sources that supports the writer's claim. The argument essay is an informed interpretation or judgment about a topic, supported with evidence that is current, scholarly, and accurate.

An essay has a title and a beginning, middle, and end. The title captures the essence of the essay in an enticing, stimulating way. **The beginning includes a hook that will grab your reader's attention, plus a claim, also called the thesis statement, that identifies the topic of your essay.** (We'll talk more about thesis statements later in this chapter.) The hook can be a quote, fact, statistic, anecdote, example, experience, or emotional plea – something that illustrates your enthusiasm or passion for the topic and will hold your reader's interest, lead the reader to the thesis statement, and compel him or her to read your essay to see how you have supported your thesis. Here are some examples of hooks:

ESSAY TOPIC: The impact of DNA testing on wrongful convictions and incarcerations

TERRIBLE HOOK: In this paper I'm going to talk about the impact of DNA testing on wrongful convictions and incarcerations in the U.S. prison system. *(This is not really a hook; there is no enthusiasm or indication of the writer's purpose and therefore nothing that will grab your reader's interest.)*

SO-SO HOOK: Since DNA testing began, 225 people have been released from prison. *(While this sentence provides a fact, it does not provide a clear connection between the impact of DNA testing and the people released from prison.)*

GOOD HOOK: Former teacher Dennis Fritz was arrested, tried, and found guilty of murder in Oklahoma in 1988 because forensic testing revealed possible similarities between his hairs and hairs found at the crime scene. When DNA testing later proved that the hairs and other evidence at the crime scene were not Fritz's, he was exonerated and released from prison – but not before he had lost twelve years of his life in the U.S. prison system. Fritz is just one of 225 people that have been exonerated as a result of DNA testing, which continues to have a significant impact on the way people are arrested, tried, and convicted in the U.S. courts. *(By presenting a detailed example of wrongful conviction that you found in your research, you have "humanized" your topic and given your reader something to care about. This has moved your reader forward to your thesis statement and presumably into the rest of your essay.)*

Each new paragraph should be indented 3 to 5 spaces. Most computers have a TAB key that allows you to indent with one keystroke. Indenting does not cost anything, and it makes your paper easier to read and understand.

The middle of your essay contains evidence that supports your claim/thesis statement – quoted and paraphrased material from scholarly sources and your thoughtful analysis of that material. The supporting evidence is organized in paragraphs. Each paragraph includes a **topic sentence** followed by additional sentences containing information that relates to the idea in the topic sentence. As a paragraph, the topic sentence and additional sentences should form a focused analysis and discussion of one of the points you are using to support your thesis. A well-organized, well-structured essay will have several paragraphs. Each paragraph will address a specific topic. Within each paragraph, the topic sentence and the rest of the sentences will provide a focused analysis and discussion of the specific topic.

The number of sentences in a paragraph is not determined by Mrs. Gorman, your sixth-grade English teacher who said there had to be at least five sentences in every paragraph, or Mr. Davis, who told you in high school that the 14-sentence accordion paragraph was the only way to write, or your dad, who said that he always wrote essays that were just one big, 11-sentence paragraph and therefore you should, too. The number of sentences in a paragraph is determined by your ability to write plus the volume of ideas and information about a specific topic that you want to convey to the reader. If you can write a topic sentence and support it sufficiently with three, or five, or seven, or nine, additional sentences, then your paragraph will be four or six or eight or ten sentences long. **A paragraph is as long as it needs to be to convey information and ideas.** These two sample paragraphs illustrate effective and ineffective paragraph structure.

TOPIC SENTENCE All of the sentences after the first one address the act of healing.

EFFECTIVE PARAGRAPH: <u>Author Gloria Naylor depicts healing in *Mama Day* as an act rooted in nature, herbalism, holiatry, and the concept of conjure.</u> The novel's many characters represent healing in various forms: Miranda (Mama Day) relies on herbalism, midwifery, intuition, and second sight to help those in need; Ruby uses her knowledge of herbalism and conjure for selfish reasons; Dr. Buzzard uses his showmanship skills to peddle his mix of moonshine and hoodoo; Dr. Smithfield infuses a small dose of Western medicine from beyond the bridge; and the drugstore where

Bernice works is the source for the mysterious "chemical drugs" that make her sick (Naylor 74). Each practitioner acknowledges the other's methods in a cursory and sometimes adversarial way, but it is safe to say that the female healers, Miranda and Ruby, are depicted as the more powerful entities. The women's abilities and powers are more closely tied to African origins and rely more on ancestral influences and accumulated and inherent knowledge than either Buzzard's, Smithfield's, or the drug store's, whose practices seem almost false or evil by comparison. *(The writer has focused on identifying healing methods in each of the characters in the novel,* Mama Day.*)*

INEFFECTIVE PARAGRAPH: Holly Larson and Anne Montz are two of about 650 students who attend the Northland Career Center each year. Formerly known as the Platte County Area Vocational Technical School, the career center has shifted its focus as the economy has changed. <u>Joanne Hamilton of the school's basic skills</u> ←

TOPIC SENTENCE

<u>learning center says most of the students are kinetic learners.</u> They have to learn by doing, with their hands, in hands-on learning situations. According to Hamilton, the learning center's focus is life centered: "Students will need to be able to write letters and work orders and be able to look up a reference in a reference book." The school's vocational evaluation center teaches individual skills, aptitudes and interests assessments to help guide students into appropriate training. Business and industry personnel representatives have a strong interest in hiring Northland Career Center graduates because of their skills. *(The paragraph has two unrelated sentences preceding the topic sentence that disrupt the flow of ideas. Once the topic sentence about the basic skills center is introduced, the rest of the paragraph makes sense.)*

This paragraph contains lots of information that applies generally to the topic sentence, but the sentences preceding the topic sentence seem random and unnecessary.

The end of your essay – the last paragraph – is where your reader will find the conclusion. Your conclusion is a restatement of your thesis statement based on all of the supporting evidence you presented. For example, let's say your thesis statement focused on the impact of DNA testing relating to the way people are arrested, tried, and convicted in the U.S. criminal justice system. You used the "Good Hook" paragraph on page 114 to introduce your purpose and thesis statement. You used the following points to build your argument:

- scientific information about DNA testing development
- frequency of usage of DNA testing in the U.S. criminal justice system
- the advocacy work of the Innocence Project organization
- examples of how DNA testing resulted in the overturned convictions of Chester Bauer, Ronald Taylor, and Dennis Fritz

Your conclusion would mention these elements. You might even return to the example you mentioned in your opening paragraph to tie everything together. Here are some examples:

WEAK CONCLUSION: DNA testing will continue to have an impact on the way people are tried and convicted in court. The criminal justice system obviously can use all the help it can get in catching the right guy. *(This conclusion is vague and offers a subjective or judgmental interpretation of the facts you might have presented in your paper. It does not incorporate your supporting evidence, and it does not tie your thesis statement and supporting evidence together.)*

SO-SO CONCLUSION: As the DNA testing process is refined and improved, its importance as a way of determining who is responsible for a crime will continue to increase. If people like the Innocence Project continue to use DNA testing as a way of revealing who is responsible for a crime, the number of wrongful convictions will decrease. Innocent people won't have to waste their lives in prison. *(This conclusion attempts to tie together the information in your supporting evidence, but the statements are vague and sloppy and in some cases inaccurate. A restatement of your thesis statement also appears to be missing.)*

STRONG CONCLUSION: Since its inception in the 1980s, usage of DNA testing in the criminal justice system has skyrocketed. DNA test results have made the court system a fairer venue for the accused because DNA test results are more accurate than older, more subjective forms of forensic science. For those whose fates were decided before the days of DNA testing, the efforts of the Innocence Project and other similar advocacy groups have made it possible to reevaluate the more subjective test results. Fortunately, for Chester Bauer, Ronald Taylor, Dennis Fritz, and 222 others, the impact of DNA testing has made it possible for these innocent people to regain their lives. *(This conclusion mentions all of the elements of the essay – the thesis statement and the points of your supporting evidence. It restates your thesis and supporting evidence in such a way that your paper takes on a circular form, bringing the reader back to your beginning idea.)*

As you develop your essay's conclusion, think about creating a circular essay – where the conclusion points back to ideas you introduced at the essay's beginning and then wraps around everything in between.

The bibliography follows the conclusion. It starts on a separate page. We'll discuss bibliographies in more detail later in this chapter and in Chapter 21.

Thesis statements

Now let's talk for a moment about the thesis statement. **A thesis or thesis statement is a debatable or provable claim about a topic, an issue, or a text that is presented in an essay in order to help the reader identify the essay's focus and purpose.** A thesis statement is a single sentence, usually found in the first paragraph of the essay, that expresses the claim and reveals the essay's direction. It may be the first sentence in the first paragraph, or it may be the last sentence in the first paragraph. Wherever it is placed, its function is to introduce the purpose and direction of the essay in one well-constructed, ambitious sentence. The thesis statement conveys information about the writer's unique perspective on the issue or text, as in this example: "The reprehensible slaughter of horses for human consumption continues despite efforts by activists and legislators to shut down slaughterhouses and restrict live-animal exports."

A strong thesis statement has "teeth," someone once told me. It tells a story all by itself. It rouses the reader's curiosity, moving the reader forward to determine where the writer stands on the issue (and whether the reader is standing alongside or is at odds with him or her.)

A thesis statement is not an objective summary statement. It is not the identification of an essay's theme, as in: "My paper is about literary little people." It isn't a dull, boring encapsulation of everything the writer hopes to include in the essay, as in: "This essay is a postmodern feminist reinterpretation of the gender and identity issues of the Lilliputians in *Gulliver's Travels* based on the portrayals and assessments of men in Sandra Cisneros's *Woman Hollering Creek.*" (No one wants to read that paper. Ever.) Neither is it an announcement of the writer's plans, such as in this sentence: "In this paper, I plan to talk about how Sandra Cisneros's writing parallels Jonathan Swift's."

A thesis statement tells the reader succinctly what the purpose of the essay is. How do you develop a thesis statement that is its own mini-story? You learn about your topic sufficiently that you can identify and express your own emotional and intellectual perspectives. You narrow your initial overly broad thematic interpretation of the topic to hone in on the single thing that makes the topic interesting, gives it life and energy, and makes it worth writing about. For example, let's say your assignment is to write an informative essay about identity theft, the technological equivalent of body-snatching or kidnapping to commit fraud or theft. "Ho-hum," you say. "Identity theft is boring. It's just a lot of facts and figures about how many people and millions of dollars are involved in identity theft each year. No one wants to read about identity theft." Nonetheless, you start researching identity theft and you run across a paragraph about how easy it is to purchase stolen credit card numbers or how difficult it is to resurrect a secure identity once a person's identity has been "stolen." Or you find out that identity theft has become a popular topic for authors of novels and short stories. Or you learn that a billion-dollar industry has sprung up in five years to protect consumers against identity theft. Or you discover that bots are at the forefront of cyber-identity theft concerns. Any of these discoveries is more interesting than the usual number-crunching, personal-tragedy narratives that bottom line with the idea that "identity theft sucks." Get to know your topic. Find an aspect of it that is interesting to you – that appeals to some part of you that wants to see how your topic fits in with a hobby, interest, or skill you already have. Make your thesis statement resonate with passion – your passion. Instead of writing the witless thesis statement, "Identity theft is on the rise due to people using the Internet," write the thesis statement, "An increasing number of malware developers have created bots that can penetrate a company's computer system and steal the identities of thousands of customers," and then focus your paper on the relationship between computer security and identity theft.

Think high energy, think drama, think Hollywood blockbuster movie as you form your thesis statement. This will benefit you in a couple of ways. It will help guide your research by allowing you to visualize the elements in your thesis, narrowing your focus to a more manageable idea *before* you start, and it will help provide you with keywords that you can use in a database or library catalog search.

A couple more helpful hints: Present only one idea in the thesis statement. Avoid the use of the word *and,* which signals that you are presenting two ideas. Avoid the use of the word *but* or *however,* which signals that you are presenting contradictory ideas. Be as specific as possible in your thesis statement; avoid wishy-washy words like *possibly, maybe, many, could, might, few,* and *some.*

After you have researched your source materials and begun to write your essay, you may find that you need to modify your thesis somewhat to fit the source materials you are using. Don't be afraid to change a word here and there; be careful to retain the passion and appeal of your original claim. Remember: your thesis statement functions not only to define the substance and direction of your essay but also to entice your reader's curiosity and interest.

How you construct the body of your essay will depend on the topic you are writing about, the nature of the assignment, and your goal in writing the paper. When you were in high school, you may have had to write five-paragraph essays. You remember: Paragraph 1, Introduction with Thesis Sentence; Paragraphs 2, 3, and 4, Body with Supporting Materials; and Paragraph 5, Conclusion. Those days are over. Your professor or instructor expects more from you than five formulaic paragraphs on a couple of sheets of paper. While the structure – introduction with thesis, body with supporting materials, and conclusion – remains the same, you no longer have a paragraph quota per assignment. If what you have to say takes nine paragraphs, or eight or twelve to make your point, then say it in nine paragraphs, or eight or twelve. When you are writing an argument essay, it's wise to include at least three points that support your thesis so that you can demonstrate that you are not just rehashing a single idea that belongs to someone else, but you no longer have to limit your paper to five paragraphs. You're in college now. You have been liberated.

Chapters 15 to 21 have more information about constructing specific types of essays. In the meantime, here are a few more things to consider as you construct your essay: point of view, word choice, types of support, and type of reasoning.

Point of view

When you write, you assume a stance – a position where you envision yourself in relation to your subject, the purpose of your writing, and the audience to whom your writing is directed. This stance is defined by your tone, writing style, word choice, and technique. It can be subjective or objective. This stance, also referred to as point of view, can take many forms.

When you write an email to your friend or your parents, your tone is familiar and informal. You use nicknames. You have a casual writing style. You aren't concerned about punctuation, grammar, and spelling. You use the words "I" and "we" when you describe activities you've done. You use slang, familiar expressions, or clichés as shortcuts for explanations. You write what you want to say and then close the note with a familiar endearment such as "See ya" or "Love ya" or "Later." You feel like you are a part of what you have written. You know your friend or parent is not going to grade you on your presentation style. Your point of view in this scenario is subjective.

When you write a reflection in your journal, your point of view is probably similar to the point of view you chose when you wrote the letter to your parents or friend. After all, you're the only one who's going to read your journal. It's not a big deal if you use the phrase *it's not a big deal* or don't have every comma positioned just so. You definitely feel like you are a part of what you have written. Your point of view in this scenario is still subjective.

When you write a reflective essay about a reading or personal experience or you write an informative essay about an interesting topic for your English comp class, some degree of detachment starts to occur. You may still use the word "I" or "we" when describing the experience, and you may use some stylistic shortcuts in your explanations about the experience. It's likely, though, that you won't use as much slang as you might have used in your letter or journal entry, and you'll be more conscientious about where you put commas and how you spell. After all, your professor or instructor is going to grade this paper, and he or she has expectations about what you're supposed to do to earn a certain grade. Your point of view in this scenario has changed; you are becoming more formal and more objective.

When you write a research paper, your stance becomes even more objective and formal than it was with the reflective paper. You are still expressing your thoughts, but your thoughts are being supported by other people's scholarly ideas; their ideas and opinions become the evidence that supports your ideas and opinions. You don't use the word "I" or "we." You use the more neutral terms "one" or "he" or "she" or the plural form of the noun that applies to your topic, such as "Canadians," "scientists," "religious leaders," or "students." You concentrate on using correct punctuation and grammar, and you make the effort to spell words correctly. You provide in-text citations and document your sources in the bibliography. You are, after all, going to be graded on this paper. You still feel the personal pressure of producing a good paper, but because you have used other people's ideas to support your own ideas, you no longer feel as much a part of what you have written. Your point of view is objective.

Word choice

How a writer presents information has a powerful effect on the audience's interpretation and understanding of the information. **When the writer uses familiar, common, or precise words that clearly identify or explain an object, a place, an idea, or an action, he is using denotative language that the audience usually understands right away.** Denotative language is clear enough and concrete enough that it does not require a lot of interpretation. It may be specialized language applicable to a specific field, but it is straightforward language that identifies or explains a specific object, place, idea, or action, as in, "A shark is a fish with sharp teeth and a voracious appetite." Denotative language does not have to be filtered through other ideas or concepts.

On the other hand, connotative language does have to be filtered through other ideas or concepts. **When a writer uses words that represent other ideas, or uses abstract terms to represent specific objects, places, actions, and ideas, she is using connotative language.** Connotative language often requires that the audience reflect on the true meaning of the word in the context of the text, and that may mean further reflection on the author's original intention, as in, "That guy is a real card shark." Knowing what you know denotatively about sharks, how can a person be a shark? Is a card shark like a lemon shark or a great white shark? It's not so clear what "That guy is a real card shark" really means. The meaning has to be filtered through external factors, like location, behavior, and the author's reason for describing someone as a "card shark."

Here are a couple of examples that may help you better understand these two terms. The term "technology" is often used by educators to refer to the mass of electronic/digital devices and systems that exists in modern society. "Technology in the classroom" is an abstract term that refers collectively to computer equipment, peripherals, Internet access, cell phones, personal data devices, video games, electronic viewing systems, software, podcasting, cables, projection

One way to remember this concept of denotative and connotative language is by thinking this way: Denotative begins with de-, as in "designated" or "detail." Denotative language designates or details.

Connotative begins with con-, as in "connected to" or "concept." Connotative language is conceptual language or language connected to other language.

equipment, control boxes, modems, and everything else electronic/digital that can be found in the contemporary classroom. It can also refer to the act of teaching students how to use these devices. When a teacher tells the computer technician at her school that "the technology isn't working in room 214," she is not referring to one specific piece of equipment or machine called the Technology; she is speaking connotatively, referring more abstractly to the whole system and all of its various electronic/digital components. In order to fix said non-functioning technology, the technician has to sort through the system, analyze various components to determine their level of operation, and fix the single component so that the "technology" works again. If, on the other hand, the teacher tells the technician that the overhead projector isn't working, she is speaking denotatively – identifying very specifically the one piece of technology equipment that isn't working.

The rose is an excellent example of an object that can be described with denotative and connotative language. Here are terms that you might use to describe a rose. Can you think of others?

Denotative	**Connotative**
rose	romance
flower	symbol of love
red petals	Valentine's Day
thorns	affection
plant	sweet
gift	beauty
fragrant	girlfriend/boyfriend
_____	_____
_____	_____
_____	_____

Types of support

The type of support you use will depend on the type of essay you are writing. If you are writing a reflective essay, you will draw on personal experience and examples to convey your thoughts and opinions. If you are writing an argument essay, you will open your paper and introduce your thesis with interpretations and examples that appeal to the reader's sense of logic or emotion, and then build your case with facts, data, and quotes from scholarly source materials. If you are writing informative essays, you will introduce your thesis with interpretations and examples, again appealing to the reader's sense of logic or emotion, and then support your thesis with facts, data, quotes from source materials, and other logical evidence. Writing an analysis essay? You will use logical or emotional interpretations and examples to open your paper and introduce your thesis, and then use facts, quotes from the source material you are analyzing, and other fact-driven data to build your case.

In every type of essay, description and detail are important. Essays with broad or vague ideas and information are uninteresting to read because the ideas and information appear fragmented and disconnected. The more detail and description you can provide, the more clearly your audience will be able to visualize your ideas and interpret your information. Be sure to document your details and description by using quotation marks and in-text citations within the text and by listing your sources in the correct style in your bibliography.

Argument style

You may have had a discussion with your parents in which they presented a list of grievances about your behavior, appearance, choice of friends, and such, as in, "Your hair looks weird, you don't have a decent job, you sleep till noon, your grades are in the crapper, you hang out with those awful kids, and your best friend looks and acts like a crackhead." They then closed their remarks with a statement like this: "Your friends are all bums. Because you are like your friends, you are going to be a bum, too." Your parents, bless their hearts, were using inductive reasoning to build their case, which they may have hoped would persuade you to stop doing whatever you were doing that annoyed them. **By presenting a list of lesser, specific details which cumulatively formed the basis of their greater, more general, ominous conclusion, they were making an inductive argument.**

Or maybe you have had a conversation with a friend who lamented, "Here's the deal: No one likes me. No one should like me. I'm not likeable. I don't know why you even hang around with me. People like me are horrible to be around." In an attempt to cheer up your friend, you might have said, "That's not true. People like you. I like you. You are likeable. That's why I hang around with you." And your friend, wallowing in her misery, said, "But I'm fat, I don't have nice clothes, my eyes are too close together, I can't play basketball, I can't afford a decent car, my job sucks. So, see? I'm horrible to be around." Aside from the fact that at that moment you might have agreed that your depressed friend might indeed be horrible to be around, **your friend, by stating a general premise and then supporting it with lesser details, was building a case using deductive reasoning.**

The same processes of inductive and deductive reasoning are used in essays. **Inductive reasoning has a pattern of moving from smaller, specific details to a broad generalization to make a point. Deductive reasoning has a pattern of moving from a broad generalization to smaller, specific details to support the generalization and make a point.** When you present the points of an argument in an essay, the reasoning pattern you use becomes an important part of the rhetorical process.

Both patterns have the potential for error due to oversimplification. You need to be careful when you use inductive reasoning that you don't over-generalize from your supporting evidence to create your conclusion. The evidence you have presented may support your thesis, but your conclusion may not hold up universally. Here are a couple of examples of flawed inductive reasoning:

STATEMENT: Cheating occurs in English composition classes.

STATEMENT: All students at Rain Forest University have to take an English composition class.

CONCLUSION: Therefore, all RFU English composition students cheat.

This is an over-generalized conclusion based on two unfounded statements that may or may not be related. This conclusion cannot be proven. Here's another example based on data:

STATISTIC: In 2006, the number of male drivers killed (29,722) in car accidents was more than twice the number of female drivers killed (12,747) in car accidents (Car Accident Statistics).

STATISTIC: The number of alcohol-related driver fatalities in the United States was 42,532 in the year 2000 (Edgar Snyder & Associates).

CONCLUSION: Therefore, drunk driving was the cause of all of the accidents in which driver fatalities occurred in 2006.

This is an overly broad conclusion. While the statistics provided here are documented and the numbers are close to being equal, they are not equal. They are also from different sources that may be interpreting different data or interpreting the same data in different ways.

When you develop an argument using deductive reasoning, be careful that you don't apply the broader generalization to each lesser detail. For example, in a paper about weight lifting, you may state as your thesis that athletes experience a number of psychological benefits when they lift weights. One of your supporting points may be that one of the psychological benefits is increased self-esteem. Another supporting point may be that exercise enhances mood. A third supporting point may be that increased self-confidence occurs as a result of lifting weights. These are all excellent points that support your thesis, but you cannot draw from these points the conclusion that all athletes have low self-esteem, are depressed, and have no self-confidence.

Similarly, when you use deductive reasoning, you need to be careful that your details do in fact support your generalization. For example, if you are writing a paper about the influence of heterosexual parents on the incidence of attention deficit disorder in American children, do not use supporting evidence that discusses the ratio of heterosexual parents to homosexual parents in families in India or describes how stay-at-home moms in Lithuania raise babies that are calmer and healthier than the babies of career moms in Lithuania. These examples of supporting evidence are not relevant to your thesis because the activities of Indian and Lithuanian families have no direct bearing on activities of families in the United States for the purposes of your research paper. Likewise, don't shorten the quotes you take from your source materials so that it "looks" like you're talking about families in the United States when you're actually using information about Lithuanian families. The truth will emerge in the bibliography, and the consequences may be disappointing.

Documenting your research

Documentation is an important part of the college writing experience. Documentation is what you do when you keep a record of the materials you have used to support the ideas in your paper. You use this record to create the citations that make up the bibliography of your paper. Documentation, citations, and bibliography are discussed in more detail in Chapter 21. In the meantime, here are a few thoughts about the relationship between documentation and essay development.

Colleges and universities live and breathe for scholarly endeavors. Documentation is expected in an academic environment. Keeping track of research so that others can verify it is part of the academic culture. Because you agreed when you became a student to accept the standards and expectations of your college or university, you agreed to document your research.

If you look something up on the Internet, write down the URL (the www-dot-something-dot-com or org or gov or edu), the name of the website (the title of the home page), and the date you accessed the site. If you look up something in a book, magazine, or journal, write down the title of the book, magazine, or article, as well as the full name of the author of the material you are using, and the publication information (volume, issue, date, pages, publishing company location, and name of publisher). If you look something up in a library database, write down the title of the article, the magazine or journal title, author, publication information, and access date. Then, when you are ready to use the information you looked up, you can create an in-text citation immediately following the information, which, of course, you have put in quotation marks if it is a direct quote. An in-text citation looks like this:

> Traumatic brain injury has become the "signature injury of soldiers in the Iraq war" **(Rand 3)**, according to a recent government-funded study. From mild concussions to injuries that violently shake, tear and destroy delicate brain tissues within the skull, increases in the number of occurrences of traumatic brain injury have been attributed to increased usage of improvised explosive devices **(Rand 25)**. Likewise, the number of soldiers who survive their injuries is at an all-time high.

The type in the example has been boldfaced to highlight the citations. Citations are not normally printed in boldface type.

You can also use the information you write down to develop your bibliographic citations. Having the documentation information at hand as you write the paper makes so much more sense than trying to find the quoted material again after you have finished writing the paper.

Bibliographies are detailed lists of resources presented at the end of an essay or research paper as a way for the writer to document the source materials he or she used to create the paper. Sometimes called Works Cited or References or References List pages, the entries in the bibliography are constructed in a style specified by the professor, instructor, or in the case of essays and papers written for professional publication, by the publisher. Generally, bibliographic entries include author name; editor name (if appropriate); title of article, book, movie, music, or document; publication date, volume, issue, and pages; and if the material is from an electronic source, the URL and access date. How this information is organized in each entry depends on the style.

The styles most often used in college coursework include MLA (established by the Modern Language Association), APA (developed by the American Psychological Association) and Chicago (named after the University of Chicago Press, where it was first published). The guidelines of each style are called style sheets or style guides. Journalists may use the AP style guide, developed by the Associated Press. Other style guides include the MHRA Style Guide of the Modern Humanities Research Association; ACS Style Guide developed by the American Chemical Society; and the ISO 690, New York Times, and Oxford style guides. Many college composition courses focus on the MLA style guide for papers written for humanities-related courses and the APA style guide for papers written for science-related courses. Your professor or instructor will advise you about his or her style guide expectations; if nothing is mentioned, ask which style guide is preferred.

An amazing number of online style guides can be found on the Internet. Bookstores sell style guides in their writing and reference sections; libraries make style guides available to their patrons. Style guide and bibliography software is available for computers and iPods. Style guides can be excellent birthday gifts and stocking stuffers. College students in the know insist on carrying their style guides with them. All right, maybe that's a bit extreme, but understand that a style guide can be a very helpful and affordable tool for you in English comp and there is no shortage of them in the marketplace. Because style requirements vary from type of source to type of source and vary among the different style guides, having a style guide reference tool handy will save you a lot of grief when it comes time to format your bibliography.

In this book's remaining chapters, we'll discuss how to do research, develop, structure, and write different types of essays typically assigned in English comp classes. This guide does not replace your professor's or instructor's guidelines and instructions. When you receive instructions for an assignment, use the guidelines in this book to help identify steps and ways to meet the goals of the assignment based on the instructions given by your professor or instructor.

What About Research? **13**

Research is the backbone of many college papers. A paper based on good research has a straight and healthy spine capable of supporting whatever burden is placed upon it. A paper with lousy research has a puny, twisted spine that can't support itself. You create a paper with a healthy spine when you do these things:

- Clarify the assignment requirements for your paper
- Give yourself time to do the research you need *before* you start writing
- Create a well-constructed thesis statement
- Narrow your paper's focus to the angle and elements defined by your thesis statement
- Keep your notes organized and document your source materials

There's a lot more to an assignment than just the final page or word count. When you are assigned an essay, pay close attention to the research requirements. Academic research is supposed to be based on academic or scholarly sources, but you might find that you and your professor have a difference of opinion about what "academic" and "scholarly" mean. Some professors and instructors do not accept papers based on Internet website sources; other professors and instructors do not accept papers based on popular media websites. Some assignments require that you use books on reserve at the library, specific journals, movies, websites, and the like. Your professor or instructor will usually include instructions indicating which and what kinds of sources are acceptable. If instructions aren't there or are unclear, ask for clarification.

Much of your research will involve usage of the Internet, the library, and various databases available through library systems or by subscription. You may also have the option of using interviews, filmmaking, photography, and other information-gathering methods to support your writing project. Various research resources have advantages and disadvantages.

While Wikipedia® has been touted as a popular Internet source for all sorts of information, it is not necessarily reliable and it isn't always scholarly. Information on Wikipedia can be changed at any time by a person who believes that something is inaccurate. You can even edit the Wikipedia® page where the editing policy is stated; that should make you a little nervous as a researcher. If the content you find on Wikipedia® on Tuesday night can be erased or changed by Thursday morning, then your resources are not all that stable; the reliability of your supporting evidence is only assured for about 24 hours on Wednesday. If your paper is due in 72 hours, there's a possibility that your instructor, should she decide to spot-check your bibliography, may not find the information you quoted or cited. Professors and instructors often advise against using Wikipedia® for this reason.

News websites may also be unreliable for similar reasons. While some of the larger news organizations maintain archival files of news articles and broadcasts, smaller organizations may do a clean sweep of the news files every day or week. You may find something relevant to your topic in yesterday's news, but it may be long gone by the time you turn your paper in two weeks from Monday. The message "Page cannot be found" is a disheartening one for any researcher who relies on the Internet.

Google® or any of the other search engines may be a great way to narrow your search to the hundred thousand or so web pages where your topic may exist. Keep in mind, though, that the Internet is filled with commercial websites, where information has been slanted (using all sorts of rhetorical devices and/or logical fallacies) to persuade potential customers to buy products and services. The Internet also has its share of personal opinion sites, where the information is based on hearsay, innuendo, and gut feeling instead of proof and evidence. Hearsay, innuendo, and gut feeling may be academia's starting point for hypothesis and investigation, but proof and evidence are its standard. You would be wise to heed the standard.

Bottom line: Avoid using for research the sites that look and sound commercialized or where you feel like you are being pressured into believing what you are reading. Websites about controversial topics such as abortion, welfare, sexuality, sexual identity, dieting, politics, and religion may rely on logical fallacies and emotional appeals as well as logical appeals to convey their message. Evidence of emotional appeals and logical fallacies on a site can be a signal that you're going to need hip boots to wade through all the junk. A research paper based on junk is not a healthy one.

Your instructor or professor may also give instructions about the usage of primary and secondary sources. **A primary source is the original text (book, article, story, poem, movie, song, photo, or artwork) on which your research is based. A secondary source is a text based on another text; a secondary source analyzes or offers comments on the primary text.** For example, you may have been studying Jack Kerouac's *On the Road* in your English comp class. Your professor assigns you a research paper on Kerouac's work in which you are to use the primary source and three secondary sources. Your primary source is Kerouac's *On the Road*. Your secondary sources are articles you find in academic journals, where the author analyzes some aspect of *On the Road*. These are possible secondary sources:

Foxe, Gladys. "'And nobody knows what's going to happen to anybody:' Fear and Futility in Jack Kerouac's On the Road and Why It Is Important." *Psychoanalytic Review* 95.1 (2008) 45-60. *Academic Search Premier.* Cline Library, Northern Arizona University. 29 Nov. 2008. <http://find.galegroup.com /itx/start.do?prodld+AONE>

Nelson, Andrew. "Jack Kerouac Shrine." *National Geographic Traveler* 24.8 (2007) 34. *Academic Search Premier.* Cline Library, Northern Arizona University. 29 Nov. 2008. <http://find.galegroup.com/itx/start.do?prodld+AONE>

"Writing, or Typing?" *America* 197.12 (2007) 4. *Academic OneFile.* Cline Library, Northern Arizona University. 29 Nov. 2008. <http://find.galegroup.com /itx/start.do?prodld+AONE>

If your assignment instructions specify a number of sources, limit yourself to that number. List the primary and secondary sources that you actually used to build the content of your paper. Don't list all the books and articles you checked out but didn't actually read because you thought there might be something useful in one of them but it turned out there wasn't. Unless your paper is about the way *Dictionary.com* defines words so uniquely that you are quoting the definitions and their origins, don't provide a separate *Dictionary.com* entry for every word you looked up while you were writing your paper. Don't cite the MLA style guide because you had to look up the format for citing a movie. Your essay is supposed to be a thing of joy to read, not a portrait of your passive-aggressive tendencies or your martyrdom in the name of higher education.

If your assignment instructions don't specify a number of sources, you may want to include citations of the source materials you read that led you to the source materials you actually used, especially if the information therein is not common knowledge. Again, you don't have to include citations of dictionary, thesaurus, and style guide reference searches unless you are writing specifically about these subjects.

Give yourself adequate time

Plan your research project. I know. That sounds crazy when you're taking five or six classes and they all have research papers due the Monday after Thanksgiving break. However, if you look at the syllabus at the start of the semester and can schedule your research work so that it doesn't all happen during the same two weeks in mid-November, you will be better off. And you won't have to live in the library. Use a planner or a calendar. Create your own "Wall of Work" (see Chapter 1). Even if you don't have all the knowledge you need at mid-semester to write a paper that's due the last day of class, you can start thinking about a possible topic and planning how much time you can devote to research and writing.

We've already discussed in Chapter 12 the importance of a strong thesis statement. As you plan your research schedule, you can also start planning the thesis statement for your paper. A strong thesis statement will help you narrow your focus from the wide-wide topic of (whatever your topic is) to the more focused thesis of (a single aspect of that topic). For example, if you know that you have to write an informative essay for your English comp class, you can ask your instructor ahead of time what the subject or focus of the paper is supposed to be. Once you have an answer, you can start directing your thoughts toward that subject and identifying aspects of your interests or study that relate to the subject.

What kind of research is acceptable? "Reliable, current, scholarly research" will be the answer you're most likely to hear from your instructor. If you are interpreting data or statistics, look for information that is recent – at best no more than a few years old. If you are interpreting scientific evidence, look for the most recent dates relevant to your topic. If you are interpreting humanities-oriented materials such as literature, philosophy, and art history, you may more likely be searching by subject rather than for the most recent opinion about your topic, so a bit of latitude is acceptable on the "currency timeline." Take into account, though, that the humanities are often influenced by cultural and social developments, so outdated research may sound irrelevant.

Take into account, too, the credibility of the source of the information you find. Is the

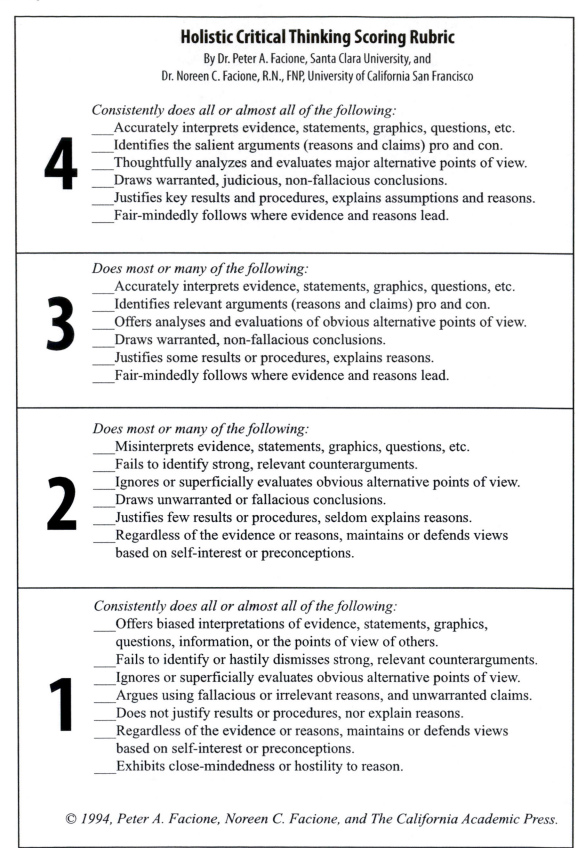

Holistic Critical Thinking Scoring Rubric

By Dr. Peter A. Facione, Santa Clara University, and
Dr. Noreen C. Facione, R.N., FNP, University of California San Francisco

4
Consistently does all or almost all of the following:
___Accurately interprets evidence, statements, graphics, questions, etc.
___Identifies the salient arguments (reasons and claims) pro and con.
___Thoughtfully analyzes and evaluates major alternative points of view.
___Draws warranted, judicious, non-fallacious conclusions.
___Justifies key results and procedures, explains assumptions and reasons.
___Fair-mindedly follows where evidence and reasons lead.

3
Does most or many of the following:
___Accurately interprets evidence, statements, graphics, questions, etc.
___Identifies relevant arguments (reasons and claims) pro and con.
___Offers analyses and evaluations of obvious alternative points of view.
___Draws warranted, non-fallacious conclusions.
___Justifies some results or procedures, explains reasons.
___Fair-mindedly follows where evidence and reasons lead.

2
Does most or many of the following:
___Misinterprets evidence, statements, graphics, questions, etc.
___Fails to identify strong, relevant counterarguments.
___Ignores or superficially evaluates obvious alternative points of view.
___Draws unwarranted or fallacious conclusions.
___Justifies few results or procedures, seldom explains reasons.
___Regardless of the evidence or reasons, maintains or defends views
based on self-interest or preconceptions.

1
Consistently does all or almost all of the following:
___Offers biased interpretations of evidence, statements, graphics,
questions, information, or the points of view of others.
___Fails to identify or hastily dismisses strong, relevant counterarguments.
___Ignores or superficially evaluates obvious alternative points of view.
___Argues using fallacious or irrelevant reasons, and unwarranted claims.
___Does not justify results or procedures, nor explain reasons.
___Regardless of the evidence or reasons, maintains or defends views
based on self-interest or preconceptions.
___Exhibits close-mindedness or hostility to reason.

© 1994, Peter A. Facione, Noreen C. Facione, and The California Academic Press.

Figure 10 The Holistic Critical Thinking Scoring Rubric is designed to help evaluate the usefulness and effectiveness of source materials.

author identified? Is the author an expert on the subject? What are his or her credentials? Reliable, scholarly research comes from reliable, authoritative, scholarly sources – people who know their stuff and present it in a credible, appropriate way in forums that are recognized by the academic community. If no author information is provided, do some research to find out the author's relationship to the information.

Even when you find current information from reliable or scholarly sources, you may wonder if it's "good enough" to meet your needs. How do you evaluate the resource materials you find? On the facing page is a chart, the "Holistic Critical Thinking Scoring Rubric." Let it serve as a guide you can use to evaluate resource materials and other readings you have to complete. The higher the score on the rubric, the more effective the source will be in supporting your ideas in a scholarly fashion.

Keep your notes organized as you research. In the chapter on essay and thesis development, I suggested you keep a sheet of paper, note cards, or a word processing file open where you can copy and paste source material information and citations, with a short summary of the article or the quoted sentences and/or phrases that you hope to use. This will help you keep track of the information you need to create your bibliography. Without this list, you'll be scrambling at the last minute to figure out where you found this or that quote or paraphrased information, and your bibliography will be a wreck.

If you're the type that prints out source materials, save a tree and read through the source materials *before* you print them to make sure they contain information you can use. A title can be misleading. An abstract – that summary paragraph that's provided at the start of some articles – may sound like the article is ideal, but you may find that the article's "usefulness" is more likely your wishful thinking that you would like to get the research done. You don't need to print out fifteen pages of something to discover that it's not applicable to your research.

While we're speaking of abstracts, here are a couple of points to consider. Think of an article abstract as a teaser the way movies have teasers or previews. An article abstract on a database provides a short glimpse or summary of the article; it does not provide everything you ever wanted to know about a subject. It may contain the article's thesis statement and a sentence or two that summarizes the article's conclusion, but the abstract does not provide the depth of information that the article provides. The abstract may be vague, or there may be jargon or language specific to the authors' field of study that can create confusion if you use the information without explaining it. Don't use the abstract as your source material or quote from the abstract. Here's a comparison of abstract and article conclusions that illustrates the point:

ABSTRACT CONTENT: Conclusion: Physicians are better able to identify obesity and its associated health risks, but some negative stereotypical attitudes persist. These attitudes affect current treatment practices. Increased awareness, training, and study are required to combat the continuing increase in obesity rates. (Warner et al.)

ARTICLE CONTENT: Conclusions: In 2001, the Surgeon General called for a change in the perception of obesity, recognizing it as the source of serious health problems. Our findings show that, in comparison with previous studies, physicians are better able to identify obesity and are more aware of the long-term health consequences. However, there has not been a consistent positive change in attitudes.

Although some attitudes have increased, there have also been significant increases in negative stereotypical attitudes. It is unclear why attitudes have not shifted with this call to action, and this represents an area for further study. Provider-recommended treatments have notably increased not only with the use of lifestyle modifications but also with a large increase in the use of pharmacotherapy and surgery. Unfortunately, obesity rates continue to increase, and further study will be required to determine what interventions are successful in deterring obesity and the actions providers can take to enhance treatments. (Warner et al.)

Digital information gathering

If you have the option of using interviews, making a video, taking photos, or other methods to research and gather information for an assignment, use an option where you either already have the skills or are willing to invest the time and effort to learn the skills before you need them. Make sure, too, that you allow enough time for surprises. Interviewing success depends on coordinating your schedule with the schedule of your interview subject and making sure that you have functioning equipment (tape recorder or video camera). Using a video camera or digital camera to capture images may not seem like a challenge – unless you're on a tight deadline, it's been raining for six days, your photo subject is away on vacation, the trees you wanted to photograph have been cut down or burned, or the presentation you planned to record that is the crux of your argument has been postponed till next semester.

Interviewing is a great way to gather timely information from sources close to your topic. I encouraged my students to conduct interviews for their career-focus essays; some interviewed professors, athletes, and administrators who had the kinds of jobs they wanted to have some day. With a little practice, an interview can be conducted in person, over the phone, or by written correspondence (email or letter). Here are some tips for conducting an effective interview. If you are conducting the interview in written format, you may want to send the questions to the interview subject several days in advance to allow him or her time to respond thoughtfully to your questions. And send a thank-you note when you've completed the interview to show your appreciation.

Interviewing 101

1. Be familiar enough with the subject that you can ask responsible and substantive questions.

2. Ask open-ended questions (Avoid asking anything that can be answered with *yes* or *no.*) Ask for details, including data or specific statements, such as "What in particular is most important about this idea and why?"

3. Record your interview, if possible. Otherwise, take complete notes.

4. Be silent as you wait for an answer. While silence can be awkward to both the interviewer and the interviewee, sometimes the interviewee will start talking if the interviewer appears to be waiting for an answer.

5. Your role as interviewer is to get information from the interviewee, not to get into a debate about the topic. If the interviewee says something that you don't understand or agree with, you may want to ask for clarification, such as "I'm sorry, I must have misunderstood that. Can you please repeat that?" Stay away from playing devil's advocate or trying to shut the interviewee down by disagreeing.

6. If you aren't familiar with the spelling of a word or name mentioned by the interviewee, ask him or her to spell it out.

7. Be sure to get the first and last name of the interviewee, and a title, and the correct name of the organization or agency he or she represents.

8. As the interview draws to a close because you as the interviewer feel like the subject has been exhausted, ask the interviewee if there is anything else that he or she wants to add. Defer to the interviewee's expertise. You will often encourage the interviewee to make a clarification or bring up another point if you say something like this: "I feel like we've covered most of the topic, but you're the expert on this subject and there may be something I'm not aware of that you want to add so that what I write will be correct."

9. Ask the interviewee if you can contact him or her if you have any questions. Ask what sort of contact would be most convenient, such as phone or email.

10. Ask the interviewee if there are any additional resources where information can be found.

11. Be courteous at all times. The interviewee is doing you a favor.

12. Say thank you or write a thank-you note.

Video and digital images are particularly helpful if you have to provide visual support for your assignment. Video with audio can be used as a source for quotes, just as taped interviews can. Allow yourself enough time to edit video so that you present only the most relevant information in your presentation. Photographs will also be more effective if you use an image manipulation software program to crop out any extraneous background clutter, straighten odd angles, and improve the overall quality of the images you use.

Drafting and Revision **14**

Actually sitting down and drafting or writing the essay should be easy if you know your stuff. If you aren't quite so sure you know what you need to know, you can start the process by organizing your ideas. You have a few options here: start with an outline, chart, table, graph, Venn diagram, web, story map, or plot pyramid. Any of these graphic organizers will help you start assembling the key points of your message.

What do you do first? Imagine what you would do if, instead of writing the information, you were expected to explain it to someone. How would you start? How would you grab your audience's attention to hook them and get them to continue listening so you could state your claim or thesis statement? What would be the most important piece of evidence you could then offer to support your claim or thesis statement? Because you aren't the original source of this supporting evidence, who or what would you quote to make your audience understand that you have researched and are knowledgeable about this topic? What would your next most important point be, and what evidence would you use to support it? How would you demonstrate to your audience once again that your argument is based on sound reasoning and proof? Who would you quote? What would your next most important point be and how would you support it with evidence? Are there any other points you need to state and support to demonstrate your understanding of your topic? If there aren't, how would you conclude your explanation of your topic? Something like this? "So that's what it's all about. If this theory holds true, as it seems to because I have given you this evidence and that evidence and still more of this evidence to show that it is true, then all that's left is for people to accept and appreciate it."

Visualize yourself talking through your paper before you write it. Try talking through your paper, taking notes as you speak.

If you can organize it in your mind and explain it, you can write it.

Early versions of a paper are called drafts; they are not supposed to be perfect. Writer Julia Cameron has described writing as "laying down track." Just as a railway worker lays down track from one place to another so a train can travel the distance from Point A to Point B, you as the writer must start at Point A and lay down words on paper, one at a time, until after much effort and many words, you will have laid down enough "track" to arrive at Point B. Thanks to you, your reader should now be able to travel between Points A and B (the beginning and end of your paper).

So start laying track. Allow yourself at least four hours of uninterrupted time. Find a quiet place to work where you won't be interrupted or distracted. Shut off the cell phone and the iPod. Gather your outline, notes, and source materials and place them where they will be handy. Sit down at your desk with pen and paper, or a computer keyboard, and take a few deep breaths. Clear your head of any distractions or pressures that might be hanging around. Start writing.

As you write, don't worry that some words aren't there for you. Leave a blank line or space where the missing word should go. Don't worry about spelling or grammar. Don't stress because the information seems to be all jumbled up in your head and you want it to be perfect and it isn't. Don't read back through the previous sentences. Don't anticipate what you're going to say next. Just concentrate on the sentence you are writing. Lay the ideas down, one word at a time, one sentence at a time. Write your first paragraph in thirty minutes, as if the planet's future depended on you completing it quickly. When you get to the end of the first paragraph, don't stop to read back through it. It'll still be there when you get finished writing. Keep going.

Give yourself about twenty or thirty more minutes to write each body or middle-section paragraph. Each paragraph should be about a key point that supports your thesis. Topic sentence first, then your interpretation and analysis of the topic sentence, then the quote or fact that is the supporting evidence for your topic sentence, then another sentence of interpretation, and another, and another. Make an in-text parenthetical citation that refers to the author or source of each quote or paraphrased text.

Encourage the ambitious, expressive writer within you to get your ideas out on paper. Tell yourself that this is working for you and you'll come back to it later to clean up the rough edges. Don't tell yourself, "But it's not perfect. It has to be perfect. I have to go back right now and make it perfect." Ignore that bossy "editor" in your brain who wants you to follow all the rules. There will be time to placate that side of you.

At the end of a few hours, you will have written all of your body paragraphs. It's time for the conclusion. Remember: your conclusion incorporates the key points raised in your topic sentences and restates your thesis or claim. You write the topic sentence, then add a sentence or two that shows how each of your essay's key points fit conveniently around your thesis statement, and then, kaboom! You have finished your first draft. The essay portion is finished. Take a break. Eat an apple. Call a friend. Look out the window. Sing a song. Study something else. Sleep.

Leave your first draft alone for a day. Then come back to it and read it for the purpose of revision. Give your paper a title that will interest your reader. Fill in the missing information in the text. Flesh out the paragraphs that need more support by elaborating on your ideas. Don't just add more quotes; add more of your analysis of the quotes you have used. If necessary, re-organize the sentences in each paragraph so that they make more sense. Rework your sentences so that they are all in active voice and sound enthusiastic and lively. Read through your new draft, correct your in-text citations, and list your complete citations at the end of your paper in what will become your bibliography.

Leave your second draft alone for a day. Come back to it and read through it – this time for spelling, punctuation, grammar, and proper formatting. This is also considered revision, but it is certainly not as intense as yesterday's revision process was. If you know someone else whose writing you like and opinions you respect who can read it through for you, this is the time to ask. Use your in-text citations to find your source materials and create bibliographic citations in your bibliography. Use a style guide to ensure that you have written your citations correctly.

Some English comp classes schedule peer review sessions, where students bring their drafts to class and exchange them with other students who read them and comment on them. A couple

If you are working on a computer, save your work frequently. Pay attention to the location within your file folders where you save your file.

Pay attention to the filename you give your paper. You're going to have to retrieve the file again in a day or two; it's always handy if you can remember what you called it and where you put it.

words of caution about peer review: Because the review is done rather hastily, suggestions to change this or that may not be well thought out. Grammar, spelling, and punctuation "corrections" may not be correct. Style formatting "corrections" may not be accurate. If you're confident that you are a stronger writer than the person who reviews your paper, thank him or her, read the comments, consider the suggestions, but use caution in responding to every suggestion for a change. Sometimes, another person's suggestions are not correct, or the suggestion was made without thoughtful consideration about the impact of the change on the rest of the paper. Use reference books to make sure that the items you "correct" are indeed correct when you have finished.

Finally, after you have made all of the changes and corrections you believe need to be made, and your bibliography is complete and formatted according to the appropriate style guide, proofread your final paper for little things. Look for consistency in punctuation marks, accuracy in capital letters and names, and accuracy and correct style in in-text citations and bibliographic citations. Remove the hyperlinks in the URLs in your bibliography so that they don't print out in blue ink. (In Microsoft Word, you do this by going to Insert in the main menu and down to Hyperlink, where you then click on the Remove Hyperlink button.) If you have used images to support your ideas, be sure you have included citations for them in your bibliography and provided in-text citations in the body of your paper. Format the paper according to the style guide your professor or instructor has designated for the assignment. Put your name on the paper.

At this point you can print out the paper and call it done. Printing out the paper is important if your professor requires that you turn in a hard copy or paper copy of your paper. Don't drag your laptop or a flash drive to class and tell your professor or instructor that "my paper's in here but I didn't have any printer ink (or paper or a printer cable) and I couldn't print it out." Don't email the paper to your professor, or say you emailed the paper to your professor, because you didn't have a printer, or printer ink, or paper, or a printer cable. While these are certainly tragic predicaments, they are not insurmountable. If you can't use a friend's printer, try emailing your paper to yourself so you can print it out at the college library. After you've emailed it to yourself, go to the college library and access your email service on the library's computers. Download the file and print it using the library's printers. There may be a small fee, but it will be worth every cent to be able to turn in a completed paper instead of showing up empty-handed.

Writing the Rhetorical Analysis Essay **15**

When you write a rhetorical analysis essay, you need to be familiar with the text you'll be analyzing. Plan to read the text you are going to analyze at least three times. In preparation for drafting your paper, make a chart with three columns; label the columns "logical," "pathetic," and "credibility." Each time you read, jot down in the appropriate column the rhetorical appeals you see and include a notation about what is at work in the appeal to influence your response. Research the author to find background information about him or her so you can determine how the author's experiences have influenced and motivated him or her to create the text you're analyzing.

After you have identified the different types of appeals used in the text, evaluate how they work independently and together to build the author's argument. If one type of appeal dominates the text, you may want to mention how that type of appeal influences the overall message. If a specific type of appeal is not evident, you should mention that, as well.

A model of a rhetorical analysis essay is provided at the end of this chapter to help you organize your ideas and information into the structure of a rhetorical analysis essay. As you write, stay focused on the types of appeals and the style and structure of the essay. Don't analyze the argument and express your agreement or disagreement with the content. One of the most difficult things college students have to learn about college writing is that instructors and professors are not crazy about hearing about the student's personal opinion or experience in a rhetorical analysis essay. If, for example, you are analyzing an essay about the impact of parental guidance on the frequency of premarital sex in suburban teenagers, don't write about your parents' guidance or your sexual activity. If you are analyzing an essay about the use of emotional appeals in political campaigns, no one wants to hear how you were moved to tears at a political rally that featured a parade with five hundred American flags. Stay focused on style and structure in the text.

This sounds harsh. You may have been encouraged in high school to express yourself about everything as a way of supporting your adolescent experience and helping you to mature. College classrooms are not as inviting. College essays as a rule don't encourage first-person narratives. Unless you have been specifically instructed to write about a personal experience or your personal views, try to avoid using the word "I" in a college essay.

Structuring the rhetorical analysis essay

The graphic organizer on the next page provides a basic outline for constructing a rhetorical analysis essay. Each group of lines represents a paragraph or paragraphs within the essay. The text above the lines describes the proposed content of the paragraph. The organizer was designed to serve as a guide. The number of lines in each section is representative of space only; the number of lines in your essay will be greater than the number of lines presented here.

Hook – Opening with an interesting anecdote, quote, fact, example, or idea about the article you're analyzing should lead the reader into the **thesis statement.** The thesis statement is a **debatable** or **provable** claim about the style and structure of a text. Do not create a summary statement.

_____

_____

Background Analysis – This paragraph should provide background information about the text (including date, place of publication, and significance) and the author (including his or her work as a writer and his or her presumed purpose in writing the text). It is also helpful to provide information about the speculative or known audience of the text.

_____

_____

Rhetorical appeals/techniques – These paragraphs should identify examples of logical, pathetic, and ethical appeals within the text. There should also be analysis of style and structure, why and how the appeals contribute to the overall message of the text, and the effectiveness of its message. Do not analyze the merits or the validity of the issue itself. Stay focused on style and structure and whether the author achieved his or her purpose.

_____

_____

_____

_____

_____

_____

Conclusion - Incorporate your thesis and the arguments/concepts you identified in your background analysis and rhetorical appeals sections.

_____

_____

Bibliography

This essay serves as the basis for the sample rhetorical analysis essay that follows.

Funnies girls: Laughing at the face in the mirror

by Susan Ferguson

Cathy is in a snit. She's met a twentysomething computer geek wearing an uncharacteristically snappy sweater. But even before the first lattés stop steaming, she's already stressing about how she looks, what people will say about the difference in their ages, whether she's smart enough to carry on a conversation with him, and finally, how many peripherals he's going to drag into their lives. Such is the life of a comic-strip lady. Cathy and the others — Brenda Starr, Mary Worth, Blondie, and all the rest — have been wrestling for decades with relationships and rewards, beauty and business. And while millions of readers at countless breakfast tables have chuckled over their antics, they may not have realized that they are actually laughing at and learning from the face in the mirror.

PATHOS
descriptive language

PATHOS
descriptive language

American comic strips and cartoons depict women's antics not only as a way of entertaining readers but also to document women's behaviors and appearances and offer commentary about societal trends. Kathleen Turner, a professor of linguistics at Tulane University, has researched comic strips and cartoons in an effort to identify correlations between comic-strip messages and messages of society. "Comics reflect the trends and themes of society, in turn affecting society," says Turner, who teaches courses on media politics and pop culture. "*Cathy* is a good example of this circular process of 'reflect and affect.' As we read, we have our persuasive guards down because we don't see the strip as persuasive. But subconsciously we ingest what we read as easily as the coffee we drink while we read it."

THESIS STATEMENT

LOGOS
background of quoted authority/expert

LOGOS
quote from scholarly source

The changes keep accumulating. Over the years, the number of women comic-strip characters has grown. So has their diversity. They may still be shorter than their male cohorts and may still have that dewy look of youth, but like today's flesh-and-blood counterparts, comics' funny girls have escaped much of the drudgery of early 20th-century life. The burden of reflecting the trends of society has fallen and continues to fall on the shoulders of young single female characters. That's changed slightly as married female characters take jobs, raise children and indulge in the consciousness-raising of their male mates, but married female characters are way too preoccupied to wrest monumental change. Their younger, freer-spirited, more energetic counterparts are definitely more eligible candidates for the task of trend-setting.

PATHOS
descriptive language/ cliche

LOGOS
conclusion drawn from denotative reasoning

Much of Turner's research centered on the 4.5-million strip collection of comics at the San Francisco (Calif.) Academy of Comic Art. It is considered by collectors and researchers as one of the most comprehensive collections of comic strips. Her research identified several correlations between society and comic strips in the years following World War I. Twenties-era comic strips featured "a whole slough of working women" focused on fashion and beauty. No one strip singled out fashion as a strip's focus, but the subconscious message that fashion

LOGOS
fact

9

PATHOS
*descriptive language/
cliche*

was important was emphasized again and again. Well-dressed secretaries whose wages didn't even come close to the level needed for <u>dressing to the nines</u> were depicted in the comics as fashion plates, and they held down their jobs despite the fact that they spent more time powdering their noses than they did typing or filing or taking dictation. In reality, Turner said that <u>during that same time cosmetics had just taken their place as a mass-market commodity, and hemlines were rising and falling faster than the stock market. Cartoonists of the era sketched out some of these changes, reflecting the social judgment of the time that women ought to be judged on appearance.</u> That in turn fostered the notion that women should seek personal definition through the use of cosmetics and clothing, and a trend was born that persists even as we approach the new century.

LOGOS
*fact; opinion of scholarly
expert*

LOGOS
*conclusions drawn from
scholarly sources*

According to Turner, <u>the single female comic-strip character didn't hold up well after World War II</u>. Many of the single working girls of the Forties opted for married life when their soldiers came home; others headed for a different kind of oblivion. Some comic-strip character unions were blessed with an abundance of children. Comic families today have fewer children that they did fifty years ago, an acknowledgement of societal trends toward smaller families. Too, like real life, today's female comic-strip character is more likely than not to have a job outside the home. Comic-strip characters have been predominantly white Anglo-Saxon Protestants, although one can argue that several comics these days feature more and more characters of other ethnic origins.

LOGOS
*conclusions drawn from
scholarly source*

In the early days, comic strips were perpetuated predominantly by syndications. <u>A series of artists might draw the same character over a period of time, each trying to maintain the qualities that make the character what it is while at the same time adding that individual touch. During its lifetime the comic strip, "Nancy," featured a simple girl in a plain black dress; it was drawn by four independent artists.</u> Nancy was an unanimated character, drawn in rather monotonous poses. However, Turner says she discovered that <u>one of Nancy's artists took more creative license, spiced up her sense of humor, and even drew a few frames of her playing soccer</u> — in those days a bold step for a female character.

LOGOS
fact

LOGOS
*fact; opinion of scholarly
expert*

Comics today feature more older single women. <u>Married women characters are usually as tall as or taller than their husbands, suggesting that the female is empowered by marriage, Turner says.</u> In adventure comic strips, the male character is nearly always taller than the female and more than likely single.

CONCLUSION
*repeats the information
presented in essay*

Comic strips were originally designed to attract readers to the publication in which they were printed. Today, newspapers are experiencing decreased readership. That means they must cater to the audience they have, offering fewer soap opera strips and fewer adventure cartoons. Even still, by depicting more women in situations that involve adventure and risk, comic strips are mirroring the activities of the modern woman. The "reflect and affect" mechanism is still subconsciously influencing today's comic-strip readers.

10

SAMPLE RHETORICAL ANALYSIS ESSAY

Every Student

Professor Smythe-Jenkins

English 100

March 4, 2006

Women's Ways in the Comic Strips: A Cultural Collage

Moon-faced comic-strip character Cathy is just as insecure as the people who read the cartoon in the daily paper. While that may seem like coincidence, it's more likely that the creator of "Cathy" and the creators of other women-oriented comics are deliberately producing entertainment that reflects society.

The article, "Funnies Girls: Laughing at the Face in the Mirror," by Susan Ferguson focuses on the research efforts of a Tulane University professor who analyzed the way comic strip artists in the 20th century depict girls and women. Ferguson is a freelance journalist who wrote for several Kansas City, Mo., publications in the 1990s. This article was first printed in *Neighborhood,* a local community news-and-entertainment magazine. The article was intended to inform a general audience about Professor Kathleen Turner's research.

Ferguson's article is fact driven and has a formal style. She relies heavily on quotes and conclusions from Turner to support the premise that comic strips reinforce cultural norms. She provides plenty of facts about the way comic strip artists in the first half of twentieth century depicted cultural elements such as makeup, fashion, and working women; Ferguson attributes these facts to Turner. This usage of facts and qualified opinions leaves little room for Ferguson's own analysis, although she does make an occasional observation. Ferguson makes a reference to "learning and laughing in the face in the mirror" (9) which seems to reinforce Turner's remark about how comics "reflect and affect" (9). She also talks about trends and trendsetting, particularly as it relates to comics after World War I (Ferguson 9-10). She cites information about how empowerment in marriage is portrayed by "married women characters... usually as tall as or taller than their husbands" (Ferguson 10). Overall, the article is heavily loaded with logical appeals.

Ferguson uses pathetic appeals in a few places, presumably to keep the reader interested.

In her reference to the increasing number of women in comic strips, Ferguson uses colorful language as she mentions "today's flesh-and-blood counterparts" (9) and "powdering their noses" (10). These clichés, however, muddle the tone of the article. The writer also uses several comic-strip titles and character names, such as "Brenda Starr" (9) and "Nancy" (10), which may serve as symbols or icons to older readers. She makes good use of example when she describes how different artists depicted the character Nancy.

While the style of the article is formal, the language is fairly easy to read and understand. Ferguson seems aware that the readership for the article is probably not interested in a lot of little facts or Turner's plan for organizing the book. The message is lighthearted and sounds like a typical book review article in an entertainment publication.

The easy-to-read, entertainment-oriented article, "Funnies Girls," brings to the reader's attention the role comic strips have played in reflecting the ways society viewed women and girls during the 20th century. It relies on facts from a college professor to outline the way comics have portrayed progressive changes in women's appearance, behavior, and attitudes. A few examples serve as weak evidence of pathetic appeals. The article is not nearly as entertaining as the medium about which it is written, but it does serve as a source of information about media's influence on culture and behavior.

Work Cited

Ferguson, Susan. "Funnies Girls: Laughing at the face in the mirror." *Neighborhood.* March 1997: 9-10.

Writing the Synthesis Essay **16**

Synthesis is the process of incorporating information from two or more sources to create a written text based on a thesis statement developed by thoughtful analysis and interpretation of the source materials. A synthesis essay is the end product of synthesis. A synthesis essay may be informative, argumentative, or analytical.

How do you decide what to include and what to discard as you synthesize? Your best bet is to look for shared themes, ideas, trends, words, and images in the source materials. As you read the source materials, make a list of the key points of each source; vertical lists will make it easy for you to compare the items you have listed. After you have finished reading and making your lists, compare the items to identify key points that the source materials have in common. After you've identified these "points in common," give some thought to what they represent and to possible relationships these points in common have. Do they suggest a new theory or hypothesis? If the points in common suggest a new theory or idea, you should be able to create an original thesis statement from them. Your new original thesis statement can then be supported with information from the source materials you used.

Another way to approach the idea of synthesis is by using a Venn diagram. The Venn diagram presented here includes two overlapping circles, each of which represents a separate source. The overlapping space represents the points in common between the two sources.

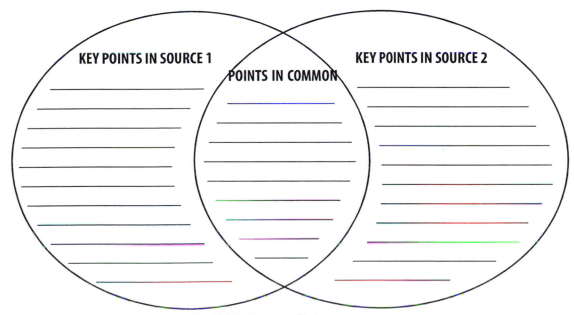

Figure 11 The Venn diagram can be used to develop a synthesis essay.

Using the two short sample essays below, we shall first identify the themes and ideas in each essay and list them in each of the circles in our Venn diagram. In the second step, we shall analyze the points in common from each list and jot them down in the overlapping space within the two circles. From there, in the third step we will create a simple summary statement that embodies the information within the points in common. The fourth step we'll take is to explore the possibility of new theories or hypotheses that might emerge from this summary statement of the points in common. Finally, in the fifth step, we will incorporate some of the points in common to create a new thesis statement that will serve as the basis of our synthesis essay.

ESSAY 1

Serendipity takes a beach by storm

By Edward Bacon, *Hatteras Observer*, July 7, 2008

Living in a dream house next to the ocean can be a mixed blessing. The 2008 movie "Night in Rodanthe" was filmed in a three-story rental house called Serendipity on Hatteras Island, North Carolina. The house was selected because of its beautiful views and its location on a barren stretch of beach next to the blue-blue waters of the Atlantic Ocean. The movie tells the story of a man and a woman's romantic relationship at an isolated bed-and-breakfast inn on a beach during a violent storm.

Built in 1988, the rustic beach cottage valued at about $400,000 has been acquired and reacquired by people optimistic that their beachfront dream house would survive the forces of nature. The house is positioned on pilings sunk fourteen feet into the beach sand, which makes it fairly stable in terms of construction. The view of the ocean is idyllic and ever changing. Nonetheless, the effect of the natural elements on the property has been costly. Storms, hurricanes, and the unrelenting tides have broken windows, decks, and doors, and most recently, flooded the septic system with sand. Originally located about four hundred feet from the ocean, today the house stands about forty feet from the shoreline.

The house, one of several rental properties along Hatteras Island, rents for nearly $4,000 a week during the summer months, which makes it a profitable venture for its owners in Pennsylvania. The owners say it's a popular place and they don't have trouble keeping it rented out, except when there are problems related to storm and tidal damage. The owners have repaired the property numerous times.

Warner Bros., the company that made the movie that starred Diane Lane and Richard Gere, paid a couple of months' rent to use the location as a set. Fake trees were hauled in and "planted" to modify the beach's appearance; many scenes were filmed at a Wilmington, N.C., studio designed to look like the house's interior. A storm that occurred at Hatteras Island while filming battered the shutters and pushed tides underneath the house – a situation that filmmakers described as serendipitous because the stormy conditions added authenticity to the film.

ESSAY 2

Ike kicks up sand, surf in the Gulf

By Jake Taylor, *Gulf Coast Digest*, November 12, 2008

Hurricane Ike in 2008 may not have ruffled the headlines the way Hurricane Katrina did in 2005, but Ike's consequences should be taken every bit as seriously.

Hurricane Ike ripped through the Gulf of Mexico over a period of several days, leaving in its wake $31.5 billion in damages and destruction to homes and businesses in Texas, Louisiana, Cuba, and the Bahamas. People returning to coastal Galveston, Texas, ten days after the storm found wholesale destruction of their homes and stores, of everything they had ever valued – rain-soaked walls had rotted and were collapsing; furniture and belongings were ruined; and water, electricity, gas and sewer service were not working. The bloated bodies of dead animals putrefied in the heat, and people were advised to get tetanus shots before attempting to do any cleanup. Utilities were compromised, with no hint of how quickly they would be restored.

Ike roared ashore like a bully kicking sand in the faces of millions. Despite efforts to protect property by applying shutters to protect windows and moving boats to safer locations, Ike's winds and rains pounded buildings and boats into splinters. Residents of Ike-battered neighborhoods are still waiting months after the storm for aid from the government to help them begin cleaning up the mess. Concerned Texas scientists have said that the quality of Gulf coastal waters and shorelines, already damaged by environmental pressures created by residential and petroleum industry development, will further deteriorate as a result of Ike.

Cuban officials said the storm adversely affected the nation's sugar and coffee industries; in the Bahamas, utility crews were sent to restore electrical service.

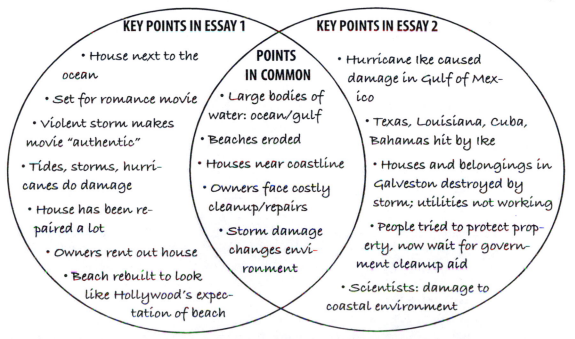

Figure 12 The Venn diagram has been used to identify key points in Essays 1 and 2, and the points in common.

The summary statement should not be confused with a thesis statement. The summary statement provides an objective statement about the points in common, encapsulating as many of the ideas as possible. A summary statement that encapsulates the ideas within the points in common of your Venn diagram about the Serendipity house and Hurricane Ike might state: "Property located near large bodies of water suffers costly damage due to storms, tides, and hurricanes" OR "People living in houses along coastlines face the possibility of damage, loss, and costly repairs to their property because of storms and hurricanes" OR "People who own houses in hurricane-prone areas gamble with their lives, property, money, and time."

From your summary statement, you can develop a more pointed, subjective thesis statement that represents the stance you intend to take in your new essay. A possible thesis statement developed from the Venn diagram lists could be: "People who own property along hurricane-prone coastlines should be prepared for the genuine, life-threatening risks that accompany all that idyllic beauty." From here you can go on to develop your own essay based on your new thesis statement, supporting your thesis with information from the two source essays. Support doesn't have to include every point you identified in each source essay; it does have to relate to your thesis.

Do you see how identifying the key points in each source and then identifying the points the two sources share in common help you to look at the source materials from a fresh perspective? As you identify the key points and then the points in common in your sources, you are essentially stripping out extraneous words and information. As you reduce the number of unnecessary words, you trim the bulk of the original essays down to a more manageable amount of information. The trimming process allows your focus to shift from a large glob of information in two sources to a single list with just the points significant to both sources. Identifying the points in common has lessened the bulk or density of the original information, which should translate to a sense of freedom so you can identify and analyze the points in common in a new way.

By working with just the points-in-common list, you are free to consider new words, images, and analogies relating to the points in common. Brainstorm. Mind-map. Use your critical thinking skills. Does this list of points in common remind you of anything? Can you draw any parallels between your list of points in common and any other subject about which you know something? When you think of the points in common, do you think of anything else that you can relate to them? What would you have to do if you wanted to tell a friend about a new theory you have developed as a result of reading these two essays? Would you identify the things in common between these two essays in order to explain your theory? Would you explain what your theory reminds you of, within the context of these two essays? Would you provide examples from each essay to support your theory?

This is all part of the process of synthesis – creating a unique new idea (thesis) from the ideas and information of other sources and then organizing the ideas and information in an analytical and interpretative way. It forms the foundation of many different types of college writing including the informative and argumentative essays.

Structuring the synthesis essay

On the next four pages you will find a graphic organizer and model of a synthesis essay based on two sources. The more sources you use, the more complex your structure will be.

Hook – Opening with an interesting anecdote, quote, fact, example, or idea about the sources you're analyzing should lead the reader into the **thesis statement.** The thesis statement is a **debatable** or **provable** claim about the content of the source texts. Do not create or use a summary statement.

_____

_____

Background Analysis – This paragraph should provide background information about the source material texts, including title, author, date of publication, and possible purpose of original texts. Additional information that tells your reader why this topic is important or why you are raising the issue will help your reader connect with your topic.

_____

_____

First point – This point will be drawn from your points in common list and recast as a topic sentence supported with analysis by you and evidence from the original source texts. Don't just list quotes and examples. Interpret and analyze the source materials to support your thesis.

_____

_____

_____

Second point – This point will also be drawn from your points in common list and recast as a topic sentence supported with analysis by you and evidence from the original source texts. Don't just list quotes and examples. Interpret and analyze the source materials to support your thesis.

_____

_____

_____

Third point – This point will also be drawn from your points in common list and recast as a topic sentence supported with analysis by you and evidence from the original source texts. Don't just list quotes and examples. Interpret and analyze the source materials to support your thesis.

_____

_____

You may have more than three points to interpret, analyze, and prove. These additional points will be presented similarly to the first, second, and third points.

> **Conclusion** - Tie the points you have identified in your body paragraphs to a restatement of your thesis statement.
>
> _____
>
> _____
>
> _____
>
> **Bibliography**

SAMPLE SYNTHESIS ESSAY

Every Student

Professor Smythe-Jenkins

English 100

January 15, 2009

Beachfront Blues: Living Close to the Water Can Be Dangerous

Hollywood may try to convince viewers that a storm is just another reason to get cozy in an oceanfront dream house, but survivors of Hurricane Ike know the real story: people who own property along hurricane-prone coastlines need to be prepared for the genuine, life-threatening risks that accompany all that idyllic beauty.

Two recent articles about storms and hurricanes bring this issue to life. "Serendipity takes a beach by storm" was written by Edward Bacon in the *Hatteras Observer* in July 2008, just a few weeks before hurricane season started. Jake Taylor of the *Gulf Coast Digest* wrote "Ike kicks up sand in the Gulf" in November, after hurricane season was over and the damage was done. The articles capture the very different perspectives of people in the eye of the storm.

When Warner Bros. rented an eclectic oceanfront house called Serendipity on a beach in North Carolina for a movie set, they brought in trees and "planted" them to make the location look more real (Ward). They paid the house owners a few thousand dollars to rent the place for a couple of months, then recreated the house's interior in a film studio in Wilmington, N.

Caro., and put actors Diane Lane and Richard Gere together to make romantic movie magic (Bacon). When a real storm blew in, the film crew was excited for the touch of "authenticity" (Bacon) that the rains and wind gave to the movie.

Meanwhile, along the Gulf Coast, residents of Texas and Louisiana were fighting for their lives against the hundred-mile-an-hour winds and torrential rains of Hurricane Ike. The storm ripped through the coastal area in September (Taylor), destroying buildings and boats and changing some people's lives forever. When people returned to their homes, they discovered incredible damage and losses that would take months to repair and restore (Taylor).

Warner Bros. wasn't at Hatteras Island to do a documentary, but the movie company could have been more honest about nature's impact on the setting. In reality, the house is located on a "barren stretch of beach" (Bacon) about "forty feet from the shoreline" (Bacon). When the house was built twenty years ago, the distance between house and ocean's edge was four hundred feet. The owners of the house that is rented to tourists have experienced many "problems related to storm and tidal damage" (Bacon). The wooden structure has lost windows and doors, decks have been damaged, and the house's septic sewer system was ruined when sand flooded it (Bacon). The owners have spent lots of money to make repairs.

On the other hand, the owners of houses and businesses in Galveston, Texas, faced very real wholesale destruction of their property. Walls were "collapsing" (Taylor), personal belongings were water-soaked, and utilities that could have been useful for cleanup would not be working in the foreseeable future. There is concern that the hurricane has damaged the coastal ecosystem, as well (Taylor). The impact on people's lives was hardly romantic as they scrambled to restore what they had lost. Many people are still waiting for the federal government to provide financial assistance and shelter to those who lost everything to Ike.

Ocean storms, tides, and hurricanes are powerful threats to everyday life, causing billions of dollars of damage. The damage can be physical, trashing houses, businesses, and utilities. It can be environmental, wiping out beaches and flooding wetlands areas to the extent that habitat and wildlife are destroyed. It can also be psychological, when people who lose their homes and property have to relocate or start over to re-establish their lives. Bacon states that Hollywood's take on a storm that roars onto a movie set is "serendipitous" because it adds authenticity. Taylor says residents are still waiting three months after the storm for government assistance to help with cleanup – a not-so-subtle conclusion that being in a beautiful place at the right time was hardly good fortune for the residents of Texas, Louisiana, Cuba, and the Bahamas.

By depicting the storm-damaged house as romantic and idyllic, and by shooting scenes for the movie in a location five hours away from the real house, the film studio was deceptive in its depiction of setting. That in turn created a false notion of romance – distorting the reality and risk of romance (and oceanfront beach houses) for a lot of moviegoers.

Ocean coastlines offer tourists and residents a welcome glimpse of beauty and serenity when the water and skies are calm. When the winds start to pick up, it's a different story altogether. Storms can pose threats can destroy property and life; that's especially true in places where hurricanes happen. While a good storm might be Hollywood's notion of a tension-building prelude to a night of movie romance, people in the path of a real hurricane probably think they're getting top billing in the latest disaster flick.

Works Cited

Bacon, Edward. "Serendipity takes a beach by storm." *Hatteras Observer.* 7 July 2008: 5.

Taylor, Jake. "Ike kicks up sand in the Gulf." *Gulf Coast Digest.* 12 Nov. 2008: A3.

Writing the Informative Essay $\quad$ **17**

The informative essay is just what its name implies: text organized to provide a reader with information designed to enlighten, educate, or clarify. Each essay type requires a different approach to the organization of supporting ideas and information. This chart, which continues on the next page, is designed to illustrate the common essay types and how information is organized within each type.

Organizing the Informative Essay, I

Cause and Effect

Describes why and how two elements are related.

EXAMPLE: The decline in popularity of low-mileage automobiles as a result of high gasoline prices and pressures from consumers.

Organization

Your essay will be more effective if you first mention the effect (decline in popularity of low-mileage vehicles) and then support it with paragraphs that describe the causes (high gas prices, consumer savvy, desire to save money, poor public image) that have contributed to the effect.

Classification

Description of the lesser elements of a whole organized into categories according to properties.

EXAMPLE: Popularity of outdoor recreational opportunities: hiking, rock climbing, and mountain biking.

Organization

By identifying the overarching topic (popular outdoor recreation opportunities), then dividing the topic into categories (hiking, rock climbing, and mountain biking) and discussing each one, you have conveyed the purpose of your writing to your reader.

Comparison-Contrast

Informs reader about the relationship between two elements.

EXAMPLE: Analysis of Toni Morrison's Beloved *as its storyline relates to her novel,* A Mercy.

Organization

By identifying and establishing the relationship between the two elements, *Beloved* and *A Mercy*, and then comparing and contrasting the features of each, your reader will be able to recognize why the relationship is important or significant.

Figure 13 Each of these three types of the informative essay must be organized in a specific way to be effective.

Organizing the Informative Essay, II

Definition	Description	Explaining a Process
Analysis and interpretation of an idea and what it means to a person, group, or to the writer.	Enlightens the reader about a place, situation, object, or event.	Describes the steps or method for doing something.
EXAMPLE: Patriotism evokes certain feelings and thoughts in an individual.	*EXAMPLE: Ireland is a good place for writers to live.*	*EXAMPLE: How to take a summer road trip across the United States.*

Organization (Definition) | ## Organization (Description) | ## Organization (Explaining a Process)

Organization	Organization	Organization
Your essay will be more effective if you provide a standard explanation of your focus (in this example, patriotism) early in the essay so that it forms a framework for the text. Then you can analyze and interpret opinions and views based on the framework you established at the outset.	Your writing will be more effective if you provide an overview of the object or situation (Ireland) you are describing and then support the overview with paragraphs of detailed evidence (low cost of living, historical significance of Irish writers, inspirational view of the countryside).	Your essay will do its best work if you identify the end result or product of the process first. In doing so, you are creating the framework (summer road trip) for all of the details that follow.

Figure 14 Each of these three types of the informative essay must be organized in a specific way to be effective.

Structuring the informative essay

The informative essay is similar in style and form to the synthesis essay. The informative essay may be based on one source instead of two or more. If it is based on a single source, be careful not to simply repeat the information in the source material. Develop your own ideas and interpretations from the source material.

Hook – Opening with an interesting anecdote, quote, fact, example, or idea about the source(s) you're analyzing should lead the reader into the **thesis statement.** The thesis statement is a **debatable** or **provable** claim about the content of the source text(s). Do not create or use a summary statement.

_____

_____

Background Analysis – This paragraph should provide background information about the source material texts, including title, author, date of publication, and possible purpose of original texts. Additional information that tells your reader why this topic is important or why you are raising the issue will help your reader connect with your topic.

_____

_____

First point – This point will be drawn from your points in common list and recast as a topic sentence supported with analysis by you and evidence from the original source texts. Don't just list quotes and examples. Interpret and analyze the source materials to support your thesis.

_____

_____

_____

Second point – This point will also be drawn from your points in common list and recast as a topic sentence supported with analysis by you and evidence from the original source texts. Don't just list quotes and examples. Interpret and analyze the source materials to support your thesis.

_____

_____

_____

Third point – This point will also be drawn from your points in common list and recast as a topic sentence supported with analysis by you and evidence from the original source texts. Don't just list quotes and examples. Interpret and analyze the source materials to support your thesis.

_____

_____

 You may have more than three points to interpret, analyze, and prove. These additional points will be presented similarly to the first, second, and third points.

Conclusion - Tie the points you have identified in your body paragraphs to a restatement of your thesis statement.

_____

_____

_____

Bibliography

Writing the Argument Essay **18**

By whatever name, the argument (or argumentative or persuasive) essay is used in nearly every course of college study as a formal, written response to a professor's challenge to "prove it" or "explain it" or "defend your opinion." Research papers and term papers are usually argument essays – variable in length and complexity, perhaps, but argument essays just the same.

A version of the synthesis essay, the argument essay is constructed much the same way: The writer identifies the key points in two or more sources, identifies the points in common in the sources, interprets and analyzes the points in common so that a unique new thesis statement can be created, and then analyzes the source materials and uses information within the sources as evidence to support the new thesis statement. The attention-grabbing hook serves as the lead-in to the thesis statement; together they form the essay's beginning. The middle, or body, includes a paragraph of background information plus paragraphs based on key points supported by evidence from reliable sources. The end, or conclusion, is a restatement of the thesis statement that includes supporting evidence.

The main differences between the argument essay and the more generic synthesis essay are these: 1) While an informative essay does not have to persuade the reader, an argument essay has to persuade. That is its purpose. As such, an argument essay must be constructed so that it will manipulate the reader's reaction or response. The reaction may be no more than reader agreement or disagreement with the essay's thesis, but the writer has to have done something to influence the reader and evoke that reaction. 2) The argument essay acknowledges that there are counterarguments to its claim. The text doesn't support the counterargument; it disarms it and then returns to its purpose of supporting the original claim.

How you manipulate your reader's reaction is determined by your understanding of the art of rhetoric. Think back to the chapter on rhetoric (Chapter 9), where we discussed the concepts of the rhetorical triangle and the rhetorical appeals. If you as a writer know you know enough about a particular subject to develop an informed opinion, that your audience for your argument essay is your wise and knowledgeable professor, and that your argument essay's purpose is to convince your professor to agree with your informed opinion, then you know that your message must demonstrate your knowledge in a way that it appeals to and persuades your professor.

People in Aristotle's time used rhetoric to convince judges to give them back their houses and valuables. All you have to do with your rhetorical skills is persuade your professor that you know your stuff and that your knowledge is worth a good grade on your assignment. How are you going to do that? That's right – by doing sufficient research, study, and analysis so that you know your stuff and by using the different types of rhetorical appeals to your advantage.

When you present your ideas and information in written form so that they appeal to and influence your audience through logic, emotion, and your own credibility, you create an argument essay that accomplishes its purpose. How do you do this? Here's how you shape your argument essay into a form that does what it's supposed to do:

- You know your subject well enough to discuss the information intelligently.
- You identify and understand your audience well enough to know which types of appeals will be most persuasive.
- You develop a solid thesis statement that indicates the purpose of your paper.
- You organize the information for your argument so that it's easy to follow and easy to understand.
- You build a convincing argument one idea at a time using a combination of thoughtful analysis and interpretation, supporting evidence, and rhetorical appeals as persuasive devices.
- You restate your thesis in your concluding paragraph, surrounding it this time with the evidence you have presented.

We've already discussed essay development and synthesis in Chapters 12 and 16. Take a second look at these chapters if you're not clear about these basic concepts. As for research, if I haven't said it too many times already, it's important that you as the writer know enough about your subject so that you can present the knowledge in a believable, easy-to-understand way. That's your ethos, your credibility, your ethical appeal. As you research, look closely at secondary sources for their style and form, as well as their content. After all, a secondary source may be an argument essay in which the author is trying to persuade you, the reader, to accept his or her interpretation of other source materials. When you read a secondary source, observe two things:

- the information that pertains to your topic or subject
- how the author organizes information to present his or her argument

Get smart about your subject. After you have finished researching or studying for the day, explain what you have read to someone else who can give you feedback either verbally or through facial expression. Listen to yourself as you explain; your diction should reveal whether you understand what you are explaining. Review the material you have researched until you find in it patterns, relationships, or other systems that make the information more familiar or easier to understand. Make the mental connections between different research resources long before you are ready to write your paper. That way, when you do write your paper, you will have a strong enough understanding of your subject that you can focus on your presentation style rather than worrying so much about whether you know anything about the content. Show your clear understanding of your subject through the use of appropriate language, accuracy, appropriate supporting evidence, and fair-minded presentation style. These actions demonstrate your credibility as the author to your reader/audience.

Likewise, it's worth repeating that logical appeals tend to be more influential than emotional appeals in a formal academic paper. Facts, quotes, statistics, definitions, and logic-based analogies and conclusions appeal to a reader's cognitive processes, making the reader think and remember. Logical appeals elicit a thoughtful, rational response. Emotional appeals, on the other hand, elicit a fleeting, visceral response that may or may not evolve into a thought. Colorful language, emotional examples, symbols, provocative tone, and connotative language may grab the reader's attention by touching his or her heart, but the reader's interpretation of your emotional remarks may not be altogether clear. If you're still a little fuzzy on the concept of rhetorical appeals, take another look at Chapter 9 and refresh your memory.

Counterarguments

Now, about that counterargument idea.... Your persuasive techniques will be even more effective when you include a common counterargument to your thesis/claim. This counterargument is usually an opposing point of view. By acknowledging there is a counter-argument, you diffuse challenges to your claim by your audience. You also demonstrate that you know your subject well enough to be able to recognize that opposing viewpoints exist.

Let's say you're writing a research paper on the importance of regular exercise on the health of grade school children. You've researched the topic so much you are doing jumping jacks in your sleep. You know that regular exercise reduces the incidence of obesity, that regular exercise stimulates the development of both large and small muscle groups and eye-hand coordination, and that exercise instructions help students to be better learners of non-physical subjects such as mathematics and foreign languages. These three topics form the basis of your claim that public school systems need to provide regular exercise programs to maintain the good health of grade school children.

As you've researched these topics, you've also discovered a "dark side" or counterargument to your claim. You have read that the quality of the food in most school lunch programs undermines efforts to keep children healthy and that public school systems are lagging behind in their efforts to improve student nutrition. You have also learned that school systems in 45 states don't teach health and nutrition classes. You also ran across more than one article that states fifteen minutes of exercise at school isn't enough and that kids need to learn healthy exercise habits they can practice at home.

You could write a paper based solely on information about obesity reduction, muscle group and eye-hand coordination development, and how following instructions makes children better learners. You could ignore the dark side of your claim altogether, which would make your paper sound exceptionally enthusiastic – and maybe a little too so. A reader reading your paper might say, "But what about the idea that kids don't get any exercise at home? Or that school lunches are full of junk food? Or that nobody teaches kids about good nutrition anymore? How are school systems supposed to provide exercise programs that help if there are so many other things that don't?"

These are counterarguments – ideas or reactions that weaken or contradict your claim. These are the kinds of responses your readers will have when they feel like you have overlooked something obvious and/or contradictory. You will have more credibility as a writer if you acknowledge these contradictions or counterarguments.

How you handle the counterargument is up to you. You might want to write in depth about a single counterargument, researching it until you can logically disarm it with facts and data. Or you might want to recognize that there are several counterarguments, and research and write about the most significant two. In any case, you certainly don't need to list all of the possible counterarguments and examine them all. Select the most conspicuous one and address it in your paper.

Not sure you have a counterargument? More likely than not, a counterargument will emerge as you research your topic in depth. Pay attention to the kinds of counterarguments (and the language that is used to construct them) that surface in source materials. If, however, you don't find any counterarguments as you research, you may have to ask someone to help you identify a counterargument that you can include in your paper. Maybe you have a friend who enjoys being the "devil's advocate" who will gladly listen to you as you discuss your paper and then find flaws with your reasoning. Maybe your professor will be able to help you identify an idea that contradicts your argument.

Once you've settled on a counterargument, approach it fairly. Research it so that you can use facts and data to explain how it contradicts your thesis. Don't be stingy with space; give your counterargument the same amount of attention that you give one of your supporting points. Finally, notice whether your counterargument changes the premise of your thesis in some way. If it does, be sure to revise your thesis so that your claim is still viable.

As your write your argument essay, also keep these thoughts in mind:

- The tone of an argument essay is formal and objective rather than casual and subjective.
- An argument essay is based on supported evidence of fact rather than unsubstantiated opinion.
- An argument essay focuses on one topic or issue that is outlined in the thesis statement.
- An argument essay is balanced, acknowledging both the strong and weak aspects of the claim.
- An argument essay is well organized and well structured.
- An argument essay relies on reason and logic to persuade its audience.

Structuring the argument essay

The argument essay is similar in structure to the informative and synthesis essays. Its key difference is the addition of a counterargument paragraph. Here are a graphic organizer and a model you can use to help you construct your next assignment.

Hook – Opening with an interesting anecdote, quote, fact, example, or idea about the sources you're analyzing should lead the reader into the **thesis statement.** The thesis statement is a **debatable** or **provable** claim about the content of the source texts. Do not create or use a summary statement.

_____

_____

Background Analysis – This paragraph should provide background information about the source material texts, including title, author, date of publication, and possible purpose of original texts. Additional information that tells your reader why this topic is important or why you are raising the issue will help your reader connect with your topic.

_____

_____

First point – This point will be drawn from your points in common list and recast as a topic sentence supported with analysis by you and evidence from the original source texts. Don't just list quotes and examples. Interpret and analyze the source materials to support your thesis.

_____

_____

_____

Second point – This point will also be drawn from your points in common list and recast as a topic sentence supported with analysis by you and evidence from the original source texts. Don't just list quotes and examples. Interpret and analyze the source materials to support your thesis.

_____

_____

_____

Third point – This point will also be drawn from your points in common list and recast as a topic sentence supported with analysis by you and evidence from the original source texts. Don't just list quotes and examples. Interpret and analyze the source materials to support your thesis.

_____

_____

_____

You may have more than three points to interpret, analyze, and prove. These additional points will be presented similarly to the first, second, and third points.

Counterargument – This point is an opposing point of view or contradiction to your claim. You can acknowledge its relationship to your claim and then use facts and logic to disarm it.

_____

_____

_____

Conclusion - Tie the points you have identified in your body paragraphs to a re-statement of your thesis statement.

_____

_____

_____

Bibliography

SAMPLE ARGUMENT ESSAY

Every Student

Professor Lee

English 360

April 12, 2007

Reflections that Lead to Revisioning in *So Far from God*

During the last two decades of the twentieth century, the image of the traditional, sturdy, long-suffering Latina began to fade – in the workplace, in education, in the media and in literature. In her place appeared the new and improved, empowered, postmodern Latina – afraid of nothing, capable of everything, and ready to take on the world. Ana Castillo's construct of the contemporary Latina in *So Far from God* reflects the political and cultural interpretation and revisioning of feminine identity from traditional passive woman to aggressive societal participant.

According to Elisabeth Mermann-Jozwiak, the novel's form – the usage of the telenovela, or dramatic family story laced with humor and tragedy – makes it literarily significant as a revisionist text: "These techniques capture the experiences of Mexican-Americans as a constant process of negotiating two cultures while simultaneously countering eurocentric notions in prose fiction. Their works show that discontinuities in Mexican-American experience motivate experimentation and ground their fiction in historical and material reality" (2).

The story takes place in New Mexico, which in and of itself suggests that the characters, and the storyline, are in a stage of transition from the traditional Mexican themes to the more ambiguous, changing circumstances of the borderlands. While the women in *So Far from God* are still daughters, mothers, and mentors and still have relationships with men or are saving themselves for marriage, they are also single and independent, or working outside the home, or lesbian, or self-employed, or (in Loca's case) socially aware but inept. Time and place are particularly significant here in light of social changes occurring in the United States during the latter half of the twentieth century.

Liberation is in full swing in *So Far from God*. Castillo's characters dispel the traditional construct that Latinas must be dependent on a man for financial and moral support. They embrace not only the desire for empowerment but the goal of achieving empowerment. While they acknowledge cultural traditions and beliefs, they also recognize that tradition is not easy to incorporate in a world where achievements and honesty are valued.

Sofi, for example, is introduced as the mother who raised four daughters by herself after her husband, Domingo, left her. She is portrayed as a woman who may have wanted a traditional married life early on, but her husband's abandonment and her reality as a single parent make her tougher, so much so that she stands up to the priest during the funeral of her daughter, Loca: "Don't you dare!" she screamed at Father Jerome, charging at him and beating him with her fists. "Don't you dare start this about my baby! If our Lord in His heaven has sent my child back to me, don't you dare start this backward thinking against her; the devil doesn't produce miracles!" (Castillo 23)

The traditional Latina role might have been played out in a scene of silent suffering or prayer to the Virgin. Castillo turns that on its head. Sofi's protest becomes not a dispute with a man but a dispute against men in authority roles, and the authority itself; she challenges the man, and the Church with its patriarchal structure.

Likewise, Loca, during her resurrection moment, debates with the priest as to which of the two of them has the more significant religious role. When the priest tells her to come down from the ceiling, that "we'll all go in and pray for you" (Castillo 24), Loca replies: "No Padre… Remember, it is I who am here to pray for you (24)," suggesting an almost Christlike identity that trumps the priest's earthly role and rewrites the traditional notion that Christ is male. Later, as Loca matures, she maintains her mystical nature and lives much like a monk or a hermit, in the religious sense. Unlike a nun, who typically lives in a more structured social community, Loca prefers to be by herself, away from people, although she steps in when her wisdom and spiritual gifts are needed.

Similarly, Fe, Esperanza and Caridad, Sofi's other daughters, behave in ways that reflect an interpretation of contemporary reality. They bond with men while they are in college, but none of the relationships last. All three women face futures without men to support them or make families possible, but only Fe agonizes about the loss. Esperanza pursues a media career and is sent to the Middle East to be a war correspondent, while Caridad suffers an attack by a spirit monster that changes her behavior and she becomes a clairvoyant and *curandera*. Caridad also recognizes that she is a lesbian, an identity that was typically excluded culturally in traditional Mexican or Mexican-American literature. Castillo tackles the sexual identity issue directly, without apology or political posturing, which reflects a revisioning of the issue of sexuality in Latino culture.

All of these scenarios feature roles more representative of a contemporary, liberated, empowered woman than any of the traditional iconic Latinas – the Virgin, La Malinche and La Llorona. At the same time, the traditional roles are interpreted against the backdrop of American culture. Castillo makes reference to these traditional images in the same style with which she pitted Sofi against the priest – not as a conspicuous assault on tradition and morality but with a clever, sometimes sentimental acknowledgement that the traditional role is no longer applicable in this contemporary society. When Loca, for example, meets the mysterious lady messenger at the creek, Sofi recognizes her as fitting the description of La Llorona (Castillo 163). However, because Sofi doesn't like to think of such things as mothers killing their children, she has not passed the tale on to her daughters. She is not tormented by her decision not to pass on the tradition; she is at ease and satisfied that her decision is right.

Castillo's use of the "family saga" (Mermann-Jozwiak 2) form mirrors the modern television soap opera, which is in and of itself a contemporary device for telling stories. That she parodies this form is like holding up a mirror to a mirror; she tells a story that is transformed and then transformed a second time so that it becomes an interpretation of contemporary culture rather than a factual account. In much the same way that Mexican-Americans have had to interpret how their culture has been transformed by the American experience, Castillo in *So Far from God* describes how Sofi's family has had to interpret and reinterpret life under non-traditional circumstances. The result is a retelling of tradition through a contemporary filter of liberation, awareness and empowerment.

Works Cited

Castillo, Ana. *So Far from God.* New York: W.W. Norton and Company. 1993.

Mermann-Jozwiak, Elisabeth. "Gritos desde la Frontera: Ana Castillo, Sandra Cisneros and Postmodernism." *MELUS* 25.2 (2000): 101-114. *Literature Resource Center.* Cline Library, Northern Arizona University. 1 April 2007. <http://galenet.galegroup. com/servlet/LitRC>

Writing the Reflective Essay **19**

Some English composition classes require that students write a reflective essay (or personal narrative or reflective response) about an experience or an event with which they are familiar. The experience or event may pertain to something academic – the writing of a research paper, delivery of a presentation, or semester-long participation in a particular course or program. Its purpose is to reveal personal opinions, growth, and development as a result of the experience.

This type of assignment usually occurs at the end of the experience or event. While it may not require research, it does require critical thinking. A strong reflective essay shows evidence of interpretation, analysis, evaluation, inference, explanation, and self-regulation. A strong reflective essay has a distinctive tone, a recognizable style, and evidence of organization and thought.

The focus of the reflective essay is personal or subjective – not objective like argument essays are objective. While the reflective essay has a thesis statement like the argument or informative essay, a reflective essay focuses more on pathetic and ethical appeals than it does on logical appeals. Facts, quotes, and other documented information may certainly be included in a reflective essay, but bear in mind that the essay is *your* analysis and interpretation of an experience and that's easier to do if you build your case with all the types of rhetorical appeals. The style is casual rather than formal.

The reflective essay can include the words "I," "me," and "my." It is, after all, a personal narrative. At last, you can set aside the more formal third-person style of the informative and argument essays and restore your more casual identity – and your personal opinions – in a reflective essay. At the same time, a reflective essay is not a journal entry or a confessional narrative. Use good sense and good taste in your choice of topics to include. Don't gossip or reveal private information you may have about other people. Be sensitive to your audience; just because the assignment has removed restrictions about "I" and "me" doesn't mean you can refer to something or someone in slang terms or use obscenities to emphasize a point. Save the slang and obscenities for private conversations. The language and word choices in a reflective essay should indicate your awareness that you are writing a college-level assignment that will receive a grade.

Finally, the reflective essay should provide details and specific information to illustrate your growth or development as a result of the experience. The significance or importance of the experience should be stated clearly. For example, if you are writing a reflective essay about your experience doing research for the final argument essay of the semester, your reader will be more likely to understand how the experience affected you if you provide specific examples that explain your progress. Compare the details in these two sets of sentences:

"When I started researching, I was unfamiliar with the way the library databases operated. I soon learned how to use the Quick Search program to look for journal articles and found the online card catalog useful for e-books."

"I didn't know anything about the library databases when I started researching. I found them helpful."

Which set of sentences more clearly explains your progress? By providing details, your message becomes very clear.

As you write your reflective essay, you may find that your analysis has broader applications. Maybe you have noticed similarities between this experience and your experience in another situation or setting. Go ahead and explore the universality of your analysis. If, for example, you are writing about your new awareness of your time management skills, and you realize that your time management skills improved similarly when you first started working part-time at your job, you may want to mention that increased responsibility at work and at school has improved your ability to manage your time. You may want to carry that idea further and acknowledge that improved time management skills as a result of increased responsibility at work and at school may be what every student needs in order to make the transition from adolescence to adulthood. The first sentence identifies the relationship within your experiences; the second sentence identifies the universal application. While it's possible in a reflective essay to shift from the personal to the universal, be sure to shift back to the personal again as you develop the rest of your essay. Writing in that big "universal" voice can strip out the details of your personal experience and make your essay sound vague and wishy-washy.

Unless you have drawn on other sources for quotations or other information, your reflective essay may not need a bibliography. Follow the instructions of your professor or instructor.

Structuring the reflective essay

The reflective essay is designed to inform, not to persuade. As such, it has the same structure as a single-source informative essay, which is structured much like a synthesis or argument essay.

Hook – Opening with an interesting anecdote, quote, fact, example, or idea about the topic you're analyzing should lead the reader into the **thesis statement.** The thesis statement is a **debatable** or **provable** claim that reveals your unique stance about an issue or topic.

_____

_____

Background Analysis – This paragraph should provide background information about the situation that led to the experience. Additional information that tells your reader why this topic is important or why you are raising the issue will help your reader connect with your topic.

_____

_____

First point – This point will be developed from your ideas and opinions of the experience. It will be presented as a topic sentence supported with analysis by you and evidence from the experience. If you are writing a reflective essay about another person's experience, you will draw from the source texts to support your thesis. Don't just list quotes and examples. Interpret and analyze the source materials to support your thesis.

_____

_____

_____

Second point – This point will be developed from your ideas and opinions of the experience. It will be presented as a topic sentence supported with analysis by you and evidence from the experience. If you are writing a reflective essay about another person's experience, you will draw from the source texts to support your thesis. Don't just list quotes and examples. Interpret and analyze the source materials to support your thesis.

_____

_____

_____

Third point – This point will be developed from your ideas and opinions of the experience. It will be presented as a topic sentence supported with analysis by you and evidence from the experience. If you are writing a reflective essay about another person's experience, you will draw from the source texts to support your thesis. Don't just list quotes and examples. Interpret and analyze the source materials to support your thesis.

_____

_____

_____

You may have more than three points to interpret, analyze, and prove. These additional points will be presented similarly to the first, second, and third points.

Conclusion - Tie the points you have identified in your body paragraphs to a restatement of your thesis statement.

_____

_____

Bibliography

Writing the Prospectus **20**

popular writing assignment on some college campuses, the prospectus is a brief narrative that outlines the writer's plan of development for a longer essay or research paper. The length and complexity of a prospectus may vary: the prospectus for an undergraduate writing assignment is commonly a single page plus bibliography, while the prospectus for a graduate-level research or writing project may be several pages long and include a bibliography and documents supporting the project's plans. We'll concentrate on the shorter, simpler version here.

Usually only a page or two long, the prospectus contains a title, a thesis statement, a short explanation that identifies the elements of the argument that the paper will address, the writer's strategies for approaching the argument, a review of the source materials, and a bibliography with citations of scholarly sources. It functions very much like the synopsis of a book – providing an encapsulated or summarized explanation of the setting, characters, and plot so that the reader can see how the story goes.

In the case of the prospectus, its purpose is to outline the plan for a paper. What the prospectus does is help narrow the focus of a paper, determine its direction, organize its content, delineate its strategies, and identify its sources. The prospectus helps the writer to stay on track. Some schools of thought state that the information in a prospectus should allow anyone – not just the prospectus author – to complete the research outlined therein.

Documentation and citations within the prospectus bibliography should be complete (rather than partial). Not only will full bibliographic citations help your grade for your prospectus but they are also beneficial when it comes time to research the project in depth; you will be able to find those source materials that you only skimmed when you read them the first time.

Annotations or an annotated bibliography may be included as part of a prospectus assignment. An annotated bibliography demonstrates that you have critically read and analyzed the sources, and gives your paper a sense of credibility in a scholarly discussion about your paper's topic. Annotations are brief descriptions of source materials; they are included in the bibliography. They may be written in informative summary, indicative summary, evaluative, or combined form (University of North Carolina-Chapel Hill). An informative summary annotation provides an objective overview of the content and sometimes the author of a source text. An indicative summary annotation does not summarize as much as it identifies which situations might best be served by the source material. An evaluative annotation offers a critical interpretation of the source material and sometimes the author. A combined annotation includes both summary and evaluation. The next four pages feature a sample prospectus and annotated bibliography.

SAMPLE PROSPECTUS

Every Student

Professor Aguilera

English 309

April 23, 2006

An Odyssey of Reconnection and Healing in *The Autobiography of Malcolm X*

Numerous traumas – destruction, tragedy, loss, uncertainty, despair, and redemption – contributed to Malcolm X's life. Acts of rebellion and self-discovery during his adolescence, and his attraction to and adoption of criminal behavior during his late teens, likewise contributed to his character. None influenced quite so much as the experience he had in prison that inspired him to educate himself for a life similar to that of his father – as an orator preaching the message of black nationalism within the context of The Nation of Islam, and later, true Islam. It is safe to say that the traumas Malcolm X experienced as a boy when his familial and cultural ties were severed later served as the impetus for his search to reconnect with his African-American heritage and bring healing into his life.

Psychologists Erik Erikson and William White have interpreted X's autobiography in terms of identity and trust development, as well as transformational change. Both researchers describe how the foundations of black nationalism and social activism to which X was exposed as a small child came to fruition during his maturation. Literary researchers have further analyzed and interpreted the roles that education (Najee Muhammad) and religion (Louis DeCaro) played in the shaping of X's youth and how that in turn influenced his choices and perspectives as an adult. Biographer Mark Bernard White evaluated the influences of X's parents, family, and environment. Their research concludes that the structure of X's adult life was set down in early childhood, follows the patterns set by X's father, and contributes to X's eventual reconnection to his African-American heritage and his move toward wholeness and peace with his own identity.

SAMPLE ANNOTATED BIBLIOGRAPHY

DeCaro, Jr., Louis A. *On the Side of My People: A Religious Life of Malcolm X.* New York:

New York University Press, 1996.

DeCaro traces the religious and cultural influences that shaped Malcolm X from an

early age and influenced him to adopt the beliefs of the Nation of Islam, and later, true Islam.

The book emphasizes the significance of religion and its role as a catalyst for X's self-educa-

tion and development of oratory skills while in prison, and upon his release, his fervor for the

Nation of Islam as a platform for his rhetorical messages about black nationalism. DeCaro de-

scribes X's prison-cell vision of W.D. Fard as a religious experience rather than a psychoana-

lytically defined event and at the same time acknowledges its significance as a life-changing

event for X. DeCaro describes X in his last years as a "religious revolutionist" who recog-

nized the differences between true Islam and Muslims in the Nation of Islam.

Goodheart, Lawrence B. "The Odyssey of Malcolm X: An Eriksonian Interpretation."

Historian 53 (1990): 47-62. *Thomson Gale.* Cline Library, Northern Arizona Univer-

sity-AULC. 23 Oct. 2006 <http://libproxy.nau.edu:2124/ips/infomark.do?&

contentSet=IAC>

Lawrence Goodheart applies the identity development model of psychoanalyst Erik

Erikson to the life of Malcolm X as outlined in X's autobiography. Goodheart traces the ele-

ments of each of the four elements of identity – surrendered identity, negative identity, funda-

mentalism and beyond fundamentalism – as they relate to periods of X's life, noting that the

elements must be applied selectively but for the most part hold up to consideration. He ac-

knowledges that prison served as a time of self-education and contemplation for X, although

he does not hinge X's life-altering transformation on a single event.

Groppe, John D. "From Chaos to Cosmos: The Role of Trust in 'The Autobiography of

Malcolm X.'" *Soundings* 66 (1983): 437-49. Cline Library, Northern Arizona

University-AULC. 20 Oct. 2006 <http://libproxy.nau.edu:2124/ips/infomark.do?&

contentSet=IAC>

John Groppe considers the Erikson model of childhood trust and its four components – hope, will, purpose and competence – as it relates to the psychological development and maturation of Malcolm X while he is in prison and as a member of the Nation of Islam. Groppe outlines the steps and stages of the psychological development of trust and how the changes in the life of Malcolm Little/Malcolm X mirror the progression of these stages.

Muhammad, Najee E. "The Educational Development of Malcolm X." *Western Journal of Black Studies* 26 (2002): 240-249. *Academic Search Premier.* Cline Library, Northern Arizona University. 17 Nov. 2006. <http://libproxy.nau.edu:2056/login.aspx?direct =true&db=aph&an=9574714>

Najee Muhammad describes the influences of Marcus Garvey's black nationalism philosophy on the parents of Malcolm X and stresses the power that his parents' social consciousness had on their children. Muhammad attributes much of X's intellectual ability and social awareness and sensitivity to his mother, Louise Little, and lays the blame for X's crime-filled teen years on X's teacher, Mr. Ostrowski, who discouraged him from pursuing his dream of becoming a lawyer. Muhammad says that X's intellectual achievements in prison and later, in the Nation of Islam and the Muslim religion, hinged on the childhood values that X acquired from his parents, who supported the tenets of black nationalism.

White, Mark Bernard. "Malcolm X." *African-American Orators: A Bio-Critical Sourcebook.* Ed. Richard W. Leeman. Westport, Conn.: Greenwood Press, 1996. 410-422.

This essay explores the numerous transformations and "awakenings" in Malcolm X's life. Mark Bernard White identifies the importance of X's childhood as the son of outspoken parents in a culture that saw the potential power in effective language usage. He addresses X's development as a debater and his efforts to educate himself in prison to develop his oratory skills. White states that X's use of rhetoric combined with his speaking skills are the tools that made it possible for X to convey ideas about black nationalism to members of the Nation of Islam and African-Americans in general.

White, William L. "Transformational Change: A Historical Review." *Journal of Clinical Psychology* 60 (2004): 461-470. *Ebsco.* Cline Library, Northern Arizona University. 18 Nov. 2006. <http://libproxy.nau.edu:3896/ehost/results?vid=26&hid=103 &sid=37ee0950-c193-4aac-9be6-71c8a404444a%40sessionmgr103>

William White describes the psychological process called transformational change, which involves a powerful change from an attitude of addiction to an attitude of abstinence and social/religious/cultural responsibility and leadership as a result of a brief, spontaneous, positive experience. White documents the transformational change experience in seven persons who suffered addictions to alcohol and drugs prior to the experience, and after the experience went on to lead advocacy or "mutual aid" movements. Malcolm X is one of the seven persons whose transformational change experience is documented; his experience, according to White, occurred while he was in prison and experienced a vision of a man X said might have been W.D. Fard.

X, Malcolm and Alex Haley. *The Autobiography of Malcolm X.* New York: Ballantine. 1964.

Malcolm X and writer Alex Haley cooperated on the writing of Malcolm X's life story as it relates to X's childhood, adolescence and young adult years. The work explores in great detail X's experiences as a leader within the Nation of Islam, and later, his revelations about true Islam and his role in the sociopolitical fabric of the United States.

Documentation, Citations, and the Bibliography   21

itations, bibliographies, and documentation seem like so much stuff and bother. Yet, you as a college writer are expected to document research sources, format citations according to style, and organize bibliographies as though you have done these things every day since you started kindergarten.

Truth is, this stuff is complicated. Bibliographies operate under assumed names, like Works Cited, References, and Reference List. Academicians and editors refer to style guides to ensure that citations are formatted correctly. Books and software programs have been developed to make documentation and citation easier. Different disciplines use different style guides. Entire courses are devoted to academic citation procedure. Would all of these things be happening if documentation and citations were really all that easy?

So, what's the big deal? Why do you have to know these things? Documentation is expected in an academic environment. Not only are you as the student expected to document your scholarly sources but your professors, administrators, and everybody else whose livelihood depends on scholarly sources to support claims are expected to document their source materials so they can be verified by others in scholarly fields. It's part of the academic culture. You agreed to document your research when you became a student.

Documentation is the act of gathering, constructing, and presenting information that identifies your research. Citations are the visible result of your documentation efforts. How do you know what to include when you document a source? In general, you should include everything you can find that would help someone else find that source again if he or she started looking for it. More specifically, the origin of the source will determine the content of the citation. Start with these elements:

- author(s)
- title of article, book, media, or website page
- title of periodical or website
- volume
- issue number
- place of publication
- publishing company name
- date
- pages
- URL of website
- date you accessed information (for online materials)

Information within a citation is organized according to guidelines set by various scholarly organizations. MLA (Modern Language Association) style is commonly used in college-level English comp and other humanities classes. APA (American Psychological Association) style is commonly used for science-related classes. Another style guide used in college writing classes is Chicago style. These guidelines are published in style guides; you can find style guides online, in libraries, and at bookstores.

When you place your documentation in a specific form into the text of your paper immediately following a specific bit of information you've researched, you create an in-text citation for a specific source. **When you list your documentation at the end of a paper to show all of the sources you have researched to support your claim, you create bibliographic citations** for all of your sources. Here are samples of both types:

IN-TEXT CITATION EXAMPLE, MLA STYLE

Castillo's use of the "family saga" (Mermann-Jozwiak 2) form mirrors the modern television soap opera, which is in and of itself a contemporary device for telling stories.

BIBLIOGRAPHIC CITATION EXAMPLE, MLA STYLE

Mermann-Jozwiak, Elisabeth. "Gritos desde la Frontera: Ana Castillo, Sandra Cisneros and Postmodernism." *MELUS* 25.2 (2000): 101-114. *Literature Resource Center.* Cline Library, Northern Arizona University. 1 Dec. 2008. <http://galenet.gale group.com/servlet/LitRC>

In-text citations are parenthetical notations within the text of a paper that identify specific information or ideas that belong to another author or source. When you use in-text citations in your paper, you are giving credit to the original author for information or an idea that supports your claim. You are doing this by acknowledging the author in an abbreviated form; this form can direct the reader to a complete citation in your bibliography.

In-text citations should be used every time you use a direct quote (the words of the direct quote must be enclosed within quotation marks) and every time you use paraphrased information that is not common knowledge or can attributed to another author. In-text citations are not intended to tell the reader everything about a source; instead, they point the reader to the bibliographic citation in the bibliography at the end of the paper. Take a look at these examples of in-text citations in an excerpt from a college paper:

direct quote
paraphrased
information

direct quote

Sara Orne Jewett is described by various researchers and writers as a woman who "supposedly embraced a female-centered society in which money was of little noticeable concern" (Johanningsmeier 57) who wrote about things familiar in her own background (Eakin 518). She was a Christian who, "like many women writers … strongly opposed the residual Calvinism that lingered in the New England mind-set long after the sect itself had declined" (Howard 376). Nothing in these authors' research suggests that Jewett was a postmodern feminist trapped in a nineteenth-century body. She was independent, hard working, and passionate

about her writing, and <u>she believed that she could make a living pursuing a career</u> *paraphrased*
<u>that, until then, had been dominated by men. Because Jewett grew up in a commu-</u> *information*
<u>nity that depended on the sea for a living</u> (Bookrags), her fascination and familiar-
ity with the natural world provided her with a lot of potential story ideas.

Here are the bibliographic citations for the sources identified in the preceding paragraph. Notice how much more complete the information is in these bibliographic citations than it is within the in-text citations. Also notice that in-text citations of electronic sources contain the name of the website (Bookrags), not its URL (www.bookrags.com). While an in-text citation hints at the bibliographic citation to provide the reader with more information, the bibliographic citation serves as a signpost pointing to the original source.

———. "Encyclopedia of World Biography on Sarah Orne Jewett." *Bookrags.com.*
    13 Feb 2008. <http://www.bookrags.com/biography/sarah-orne-jewett/>

Eakin, Paul John. "Sarah Orne Jewett and the Meaning of Country Life." *American*
    Literature 38:4 508-531. *JSTOR.* Cline Library, Northern Arizona
    University. 8 Feb 2008. <http://links.jstor.org/sici?sici=0002-
    9831%28196701%2938%3A4%3C508%3ASOJATM%3E2.0.CO%3B2-C>

Howard, June. "Unraveling Regions, Unsettling Periods: Sarah Orne Jewett and
    American Literary History." *American Literature* 68:2 365-384.
    JSTOR. Cline Library, Northern Arizona University. 12 Feb 2008.
    <http://links.jstor.org/sici?sici=0002-9831%28199606%2968%3A
    2%3C365%3AURUPSO%3E2.0.CO%3B2-G>

Johanningsmeier, Charles. "Sarah Orne Jewett and Mary E. Wilkins (Freeman): Two
    Shrewd Businesswomen in Search of New Markets." *The New England*
    Quarterly 70:1 57-82. *JSTOR.* Cline Library, Northern Arizona University.
    8 Feb. 2008. <http://links.jstor.org/sici?sici=00284866%28199703%2970%3
    A1%3C57%3ASOJAME%3E2.0.CO%3B2-0>

Remember, in-text citations should have sufficient information to point your reader to the bibliographic citation which, in turn, points to the original source. All citations should be written according to the specific style guide (MLA, APA, Chicago, or other) that meets the expectations of the assignment and your professor or instructor.

When you organize citations to make the perfect bibliography, you assemble them alphabetically according to author's last name or, if there is no author, the first major word of the title.

That in a nutshell is documentation, citation, and bibliography. And that, in a nutshell, is how to pass English comp. American historian Will Durant said at some point in his life that "education is a progressive discovery of our own ignorance." I hope you have gleaned something from this book that has helped you to recognize your own ignorance and that this book has provided you with the tools to fix it. Now get out there. Do great things. The world is waiting.

Bibliography/Credits/Permissions

Adapted from *Mockingbird: A Portrait of Harper Lee* by Charles J. Shields. Copyright ©
2006 by Charles J. Shields. Additional material copyright © 2007 by Charles J.
Shields. Reprinted by permission of Henry Holt and Company, LLC.

"Annotated Bibliographies." *Handouts and Links: The Writing Center, University of
North Carolina at Chapel Hill.* 4 Dec. 2008. <http://www.unc.edu/depts/wcweb/hand-
outs/annotated_bibliographies.html>

Aristotle. *The Art of Rhetoric.* Trans. John Henry Freese. London. 1926. *Internet Archive.* 21
Oct. 2008. <http://www.archive.org/details/artofrhetoric00arisuoft>

"Arizona Academic Standards." *Arizona Department of Education: Writing Standards
Articulated by Grade Level.* 30 Oct. 2008. <http//:www.ade.state.az.us:standards:lan-
guage-arts:writing:articulated.asp> Reprinted with permission of Arizona Department
of Education.

Barrow Neurological Institute. *Traumatic Brain Injury Guidebook.* 2 Sept. 2008.
<www.thebarrow.org/Medical_Specialties_Centers_and_Clinics/Neurotrauma_Prog
ram/Traumatic_Brain_Injury/index.htm?ssSourceNodeId=5012473&ssSource
SiteId=50 12151>

Bullock, Richard. *The Norton Field Guide to Writing.* New York: W.W. Norton & Company,
2006.

Buranen, Lisa, and Alice Myers Roy. *Perspectives on Plagiarism and Intellectual Property in
a Postmodern World.* Albany: State University of New York Press, 1999. 13 Nov. 2008.
<http://books.google.com/books?id=jSSBzCskVZQC>

"Car Accident Statistics." *Car-Accidents.com.* 21 Nov. 2008.
<http://www.car-accidents.com/pages/car-crash-men-woman.html>

"DNA Forensics: Expanding Uses and Information Sharing." *Bureau of Justice Statistics.*
24 Nov. 2008. <http://www.ojp.usdoj.gov/bjs/abstract/dnaf.htm>

"Drunk Driving Accident Statistics." *Edgar Snyder & Associates.* 24 Nov. 2008.
<http://www.edgarsnyder.com/auto-accident/drunk-driving/statistics.html>

Durant, Will. Quote. *The Quotations Page.* 13 Dec. 2008.
<http://www.quotationspage.com/quotes/Will_Durant/>

"Elizabeth Ewen." *BarnesandNoble.com.* 8 Dec. 2008.
<http://search.barnesandnoble.com/Typecasting/Stuart-Ewen/e/9781583227350>

"Essayplant.com: Term Paper, Essay, Research Company-No Plagiarism."
Essayplant.com. 11 Nov. 2008. <http://essayplant.com/noplagiarism.php>

Ewen, Stuart and Elizabeth Ewen. *Channels of Desire.* Minneapolis: University of Minnesota
Press, 1982. Reprinted by permission of the University of Minnesota.

Facione, Peter A. "Critical Thinking: What It Is and Why It Counts." *Insight Assessment/The California Academic Press.* 29 Oct. 2008. <http://www.insightassessment.com/9arti cles%20WW.html> Originally published in Millbrae, CA., by Insight Assessment /The California Academic Press. Reprinted with permission.

Facione, Peter A., and Noreen C. Facione. "Holistic Critical Thinking Scoring Rubric." *Insight Assessment/The California Academic Press.* 29 Oct. 2008. <http://www.insigh tassessment.com/> Originally published in Millbrae, CA., by Insight Assessment /The California Academic Press. Reprinted with permission.

Ferguson, Susan. "Does feminism fly as a foundation in Jewett's 'A White Heron'?" Northern Arizona University. 14 Feb. 2008.

---. "An Odyssey of Reconnection and Healing in *The Autobiography of Malcolm X.*" Northern Arizona University. 12 Dec. 2006.

---. "Matriarchal healing in *Mama Day.*" Northern Arizona University. 26 Sept. 2006.

---. "Reflections that lead to revisioning in *So Far from God.*" Northern Arizona University. 24 March 2008.

---. "Traumatic brain injury affects Iraq War veterans." Sedona, AZ. 12 Nov. 2008.

"The Flesch Reading Ease Readability Formula." *Readability Formulas.com.* 12 Nov. 2008. <http://www.readabilityformulas.com/flesch-reading-ease-readability-formula.php>

Fralic, Shelley. "Serendipity steals the show in film romance." *The Vancouver Sun.* 10 Oct. 2008. 29 Nov. 2008. <http://www.canada.com/vancouversun/columnists/story.html ?id=fbcd087b-2041-41d6-a7c4-02b507ab6f88>

Frank, Marc. "Cuba counts up damage from Hurricane Ike." *Caribbean Net News.* 11 Sept. 2008. 29 Nov. 2008. <http://www.caribbeannetnews.com/article.php?news–id=10589.>

Fritz, Dennis. *Journey Toward Justice.* Santa Ana, CA: Seven Locks Press, 2006.

"Grand Bahama Power linesmen return from Hurricane Ike restoration efforts." *Bahama Islands Info.* 4 Nov. 2008. 29 Nov. 2008. <http://www.bahamaislandsinfo.com/index. php?option=com_content&view=article&catid=33:News%20&%20Info%20about %20Grand%20Bahama&id=1834:grand-bahama-power-linesmen-return-from-hurricane-ike-restoration-efforts&Itemid=146>

Gray-Rosendale, Laura. *Pop Perspectives: Readings to Critique Contemporary Culture.* Boston: McGraw Hill, 2007.

Hacker, Diana. *A Pocket Style Manual: Fourth Edition.* Boston: Bedford/St. Martin's, 2004.

Hagerman, Eric. "Shock to the System." *Popular Science.* 27 Sept. 2008. <http://www.popsci.com/military-aviation-%2526-space/article/2008-08/shock-sys tem>

Holt, Tim. "Logical Fallacies.info." *Logical Fallacies.info.* 21 Nov 2008. <http://www.logi-calfallacies.info/>

"How Occam's Razor Works." *How Stuff Works.* 12 Dec. 2008. <http://people.how stuffworks.com/occams-razor.html>

"Howard Gardner, multiple intelligences and education." *The encyclopedia of informal education.* 14 Nov. 2008. <http://www.infed.org/thinkers/gardner.htm>

Kozak, Catherine. "Outer Banks home plays starring role in new film." *Pilot Online.com.* 26 Sept. 2008. 29 Nov. 2008. <http://hamptonroads.com/2008/09/weather-clouds-debut-outer-banks-cottage-nights-rodanthe>

Loftis, Randy Lee. "Hurricane Ike further damages Texas' fragile coastal ecosystem." *Dallas*

Morning News. 17 Sept. 2008. 29 Nov. 2008. <http://www.dallasnews.com/sharedcon tent/dws/fea/greenliving/stories/091708dntexikeeco.19d2dc7.html>

Luskin, Casey. "Is the Latest 'Feathered Dinosaur' Actually a Secondarily Flightless Bird?" *Evolution News and Views*. 22 Nov. 2008. <http://www.evolutionnews.org/2008/ 11/is_the_latest_feathered_dinosa.html>

"Mission Statement." *The Innocence Project*. 24 Nov. 2008. <http://www.innocence project.org/about/Mission-Statement.php>

Nolan, Irene. "The mess at Mirlo Beach." *Island Free Press*. 29 Nov. 2008. <http://www.islandfreepress.org/Archives/2007.11.29-ShootingTheBreeze-MirloBeach.html>

"Paper Masters: Term Papers-Custom Research Papers." *Paper Masters*. 11 Nov. 2008. <http://www.papermasters.com/>

Paul, Richard, and Linda Elder. *A Guide for Educators to Critical Thinking Competency Standards*. Dillon Beach, CA: Foundation for Critical Thinking. 14 Nov. 2008. <http://books.google.com/books?id=wAZHakBsYIgC>

"Questions to Ask for a Critical Reading." *University of British Columbia Writing Centre*. 29 Oct. 2008. <http://www.writingcentre.ubc.ca/workshop/tools/rhet1.htm> Reprinted by permission of the University of British Columbia Writing Centre.

"Storm-Battered Galveston Residents Return Home." *The Weather Channel*. 29 Nov. 2008. <http://www.weatherplus.com/hurricane-central-features/storm-battered-galveston-allow.php>

"Stuart Ewen." *NYU Libraries-Tamiment Library & Robert F. Wagner Labor Archives*. 8 Dec. 2008. <http://www.nyu.edu/library/bobst/research/tam/ewen/stuart_ewen.html>

Tanielian, Terry, and Lisa H. Jaycox, Eds. *Invisible Wounds of War: Psychological and Cognitive Injuries, Their Consequences, and Services to Assist Recovery*. 27 Sept. 2008. <http://www.rand.org>

Tarantino, Quentin and Roger Avary. *Pulp Fiction*. 14 Dec. 2008. <www.imsdb.com/scripts/Pulp-Fiction.html>

"Undergraduate Admissions." *Northern Arizona University–Admission Requirements*. 6 Nov. 2008. <http://home.nau.edu/admissions/apply/admissreq.asp>

"Understanding Stress." *HelpGuide*. 12 Nov. 2008. <http://www.helpguide.org/mental/stress_signs.htm>

Warner, Christopher, Carolynn M. Warner, Joshua Morganstein, George N. Appenzeller, James Rachat, and Thomas Grieger. "Military Family Physician Attitudes toward Treating Obesity." *Military Medicine* 173:10 (2008) 978. 26 Nov. 2008. *Ebscohost*. Cline Library, Northern Arizona University.

"What Is Plagiarism? Gervase Programs: Learning to Lead." *Georgetown University*. 9 Dec. 2008. <http://gervaseprograms.georgetown.edu/honor/system/53377.html>

Index